I dedicate this book to Alysha Waters, who rode life's other merry-go-round as we both reached for the golden ring.

About the Author

Jim Tolpin has operated a finish carpentry and custom cabinetmaking business since 1969. He has written numerous books on the woodworking trade including *Measure Twice, Cut Once; Building Traditional Kitchen Cabinets; Jim Tolpin's Table Saw Magic;* and *Jim Tolpin's Woodworking Wit & Wisdom.*

Acknowledgements

I wish to acknowledge the following good people, who, sometimes unwittingly, taught me something I needed to know: Sam Rosoff, Irving Pregozen, Jay Leech, Ludwig Furtner, Warren Wilson, John Muxie, Steven Souder, Johnny Coyne, Frank Whittemore, David Sawyer, Doug Fowle, Dan Valenza, Bud McIntosh, Diane Gusset, Ken Kellman, Daniel Neville, John Ewald, Chris Marrs, Charles Landau, John Maurer and Walter and Susan Melton. If not for them, I'd still be holding the dumb end of the tape. Special thanks to cabinetmaker John Marckworth for loaning us some tools, his shop and even his person for some of the photography and to Seb Eggert of Maisefield Mantels for loaning us his entire shop for a couple of hours for a photo shoot!

I am especially indebted to Francis "Nat" Natali, who showed me that learning to write is not unlike learning to ride a bicycle — "Just keep at it and you'll find that the balance comes of its own" — and to Laura Tringali, who kicked off the training wheels. At F+W Publications, thanks to Jim Stack, David Lewis and all the others who helped bring this book to market. Finally, I wish to thank photographers Pat Cudahy and Craig Wester for their skills and perseverance.

table of contents

Jim Tolpin's Guide to Becoming a

Professional Cabinetmaker

POPULAR WOODWORKING BOOKS
CINCINNATI, OHIO
www.popularwoodworking.com

Read This Important Safety Notice

To prevent accidents, keep safety in mind while you work. Use the safety guards installed on power equipment; they are for your protection. When working on power equipment, keep fingers away from saw blades, wear safety goggles to prevent injuries from flying wood chips and sawdust and wear headphones to protect your hearing. Consider installing a dust vacuum to reduce the amount of airborne sawdust in your woodshop. Don't wear loose clothing, such as neckties or loose-sleeved shirts, or jewelry, such as rings, necklaces or bracelets, when working on power equipment. Tie back long hair to prevent it from getting caught in your equipment. People who are sensitive to certain chemicals should check the chemical content of any product before using it. The authors and editors who compiled this book have tried to make the contents as accurate and correct as possible. Plans, illustrations, photographs and text have been carefully checked. All instructions, plans and projects should be carefully read, studied and understood before beginning construction. In some photos, power tool guards have been removed to more clearly show the operation being demonstrated. Always use all safety guards and attachments that come with your power tools. Due to the variability of local conditions, construction materials, skill levels, etc., neither the author nor Popular Woodworking Books assumes any responsibility for any accidents, injuries, damages or other losses incurred resulting from the material presented in this book. Prices listed for supplies and equipment were current at the time of publication and are subject to change. Glass shelving should have all edges polished and must be tempered. Untempered glass shelves may shatter and can cause serious bodily injury. Tempered shelves are very strong; if they break they will just crumble, minimizing personal injury.

Jim Tolpin's Guide to Becoming a Professional Cabinetmaker. Copyright © 2005 by Jim Tolpin. Printed and bound in China. All rights reserved. No part of this book may be reproduced in any form or by any electronic or mechanical means including information storage and retrieval systems without permission in writing from the publisher, except by a reviewer, who may quote brief passages in a review. Published by Popular Woodworking Books, an imprint of F+W Publications, Inc., 4700 East Galbraith Road, Cincinnati, Ohio 45236. First edition.

Distributed in Canada by Fraser Direct
100 Armstrong Avenue
Georgetown, Ontario L7G 5S4
Canada

Distributed in the U.K. and Europe by David & Charles
Brunel House
Newton Abbot
Devon TQ12 4PU
England
Tel: (+44) 1626 323200
Fax: (+44) 1626 323319
E-mail: mail@davidandcharles.co.uk

Distributed in Australia by Capricorn Link
P.O. Box 704
Windsor, NSW 2756
Australia

Visit our Web site at www.popularwoodworking.com for information on more resources for woodworkers.

Other fine Popular Woodworking Books are available from your local bookstore or direct from the publisher.

09 08 07 06 05   5 4 3 2 1

Library of Congress Cataloging-in-Publication Data

Tolpin, Jim, 1947-
    Jim Tolpin's guide to becoming a professional cabinetmaker / Jim Tolpin.
        p.   cm.
    Includes index.
    ISBN 1-55870-753-0 (pbk: alk. paper)
    1. Workshops.   2. Cabinetwork.   3. Cabinetmakers.   I. Title: Guide to becoming a professional cabinetmaker.   II. Title.
TT152.T65   2005
684.1'.04--dc22   2005003054

ACQUISITIONS EDITOR: Jim Stack
EDITOR: Amy Hattersley
DESIGNER: Brian Roeth
ILLUSTRATOR: Len Churchill
LAYOUT ARTIST: Kathy Gardner
COVER PHOTOGRAPHER: Tim Grondin
PRODUCTION COORDINATOR: Jennifer Wagner

F+W PUBLICATIONS, INC.

introduction

IT'S BEEN MORE THAN 30 YEARS SINCE I FIRST started working at woodworking. In the beginning, I worked alone in a one-car garage outfitted with a minimal number of tools. Today I am the sole proprietor of a one-man cabinet shop, and I work out of a two-car garage outfitted with a minimal number of tools.

"That boy's gone far," I can hear you saying. "Now he has room for a second car." There is, however, an even greater difference: This boy can now afford a second car. In my first 10 years of working wood for a living, I could barely provide for myself or the family of four I now support (another difference 30 years can make), let alone a second car. It was not the woodworking itself but the way in which I was working the wood that forestalled my financial success.

During those first 10 years, I often built highly refined pieces of casework that required much hand joinery and tedious fine detailing. I called the results of these efforts kitchen cabinets. With each delivery, I bathed in my clientele's enthusiastic approval of my work. Little did I realize how much of the celebration was due to their joy at obtaining such a piece at such a price — at least not until the day I looked up from my work and realized that this was not cabinetmaking. I was going broke like nearly every custom furniture maker I had ever met. It had come time to unplug myself from the shop for a while and try to figure out what I was doing wrong.

Before long, I had three likely answers. First, I did not have the faintest idea about how to build cabinets — in fact, I didn't really know what a kitchen cabinet was. Second, my methods and tooling, such as they were, were primitive and counterproductive. Third, I was an abysmally poor businessman. To continue practicing woodworking as a livelihood, I had to understand the market's perspective of a quality piece of cabinetry and learn how to build it as efficiently as possible. I also had to learn how to successfully present myself and my products to the public.

I began my education by taking a long, hard look at top-of-the-line cabinetry on display at several local showrooms. I quickly found that I had a great deal to learn from the products imported from Europe. With childlike awe, I examined the incredibly sophisticated hardware system that allowed these cabinets to achieve fitting tolerances generally unheard of in kitchen cabinetry. Looking closer, I learned that the casework was manufactured so that any variety of hardware elements could be installed: A cabinet module could hold numerous configurations of doors, drawers and shelving without further processing. My mind boggled at the implications this would have on my primitive approach to cabinetmaking.

Imbued with a new vision of the cabinetry I would strive to produce, I turned my attention to my shop. It would be necessary to revamp the layout of the work space completely and to upgrade the tools. Out went dust-collecting workbenches and an ancient, massive surface planer. I brought in mobile caddies, for tools and materials, and a multipurpose knockdown work platform. I hung a new, lightweight planer from the ceiling, instantly ready for use with a heave on a rope. I regrouped the major stationary tools into symbiotic clusters, creating compact workstations. I also upgraded the table saw, radial-arm saw and drill press with new fence systems, which practically eliminated the need for a tape measure during sizing and milling operations.

With the physical plant in shape, I focused my attention on the production process itself. I analyzed the way in which materials flowed through the shop and how processes could be grouped and sequenced. I mapped out a plan that would make the most of my time and my modest floor space. The end result was the creation of a production flowchart that carried me smoothly from the initial stages of developing the layout and cut lists through the production process to the instal-

Photo credit:
Craig Wester
Cabinets designed
and built by John
Marckworth and
Jim Tolpin.

plored the paper trail that must be followed to lend a bureaucrat's vision of credibility to a small business. I researched the legal ramifications of the various forms a business might take. I became acutely aware of the art of image-making. Dealing with clients, I not only learned how to clean up my act, I made one up. Finally, I designed a paperwork system specifically for small-shop cabinetmaking, and it simplified the day-to-day documentation of production data and business transactions.

lation of the product on site.

At this point, I had a firm grasp of the products I intended to offer the market, and I had a revitalized shop and work style. I needed to jump one remaining hurdle: the world of business. The task of creating a viable business enterprise struck me as something intangible and daunting. I soon realized, however, that I needed only to apply the same frame of mind that had wrought such miraculous changes in my shop.

I began by talking with people who were operating small businesses like mine, but successfully, and I quickly learned what I needed to do. I ex-

This book is divided into the three major areas I worked on to fix what was going wrong with my career: the shop, the process and the business. Together they comprise the story of how I now go about making a living at woodworking. It's the story of working hard, working well and producing a product whose market value amply rewards its maker. I am thankful to have been able to write this book. Who knows, if I hadn't looked up from my work that fateful day, things might be different. I probably would have ended up going back to college for an advanced degree and would now be stuck with a real job. I shudder to think. . . .

the shop

NOTHING IS PROBABLY MORE SUBJECTIVE IN the mind of cabinetmakers than the idea of what constitutes a perfect shop. Your perfect shop will be one that works with you on a daily basis to help you create a product in an efficient, enjoyable manner. If your shop doesn't do this, it's worth your time and energy to change it so that it does.

The shop I currently work in is not large by many cabinetmaker's standards; it's basically a two-car garage with the blessing of a 10'-high ceiling. I have learned, however, through years of coping with various spaces — most even smaller than this one — that size is not the single determining factor for a workable environment. Other factors to consider (and believe me, we will) are efficient use of floor space, orientation of the major stationary tools and workstations, careful management of material flow through the shop, and proper sequencing of production processes.

Over the past two decades, two basic rules have evolved for me as a result of life in these small spaces. The first rule is this: *Nothing gets to occupy the shop's floor space except the essential stationary power tools.* Bikes, washing machines, camping gear and useless tools are no longer tolerated in my work space. To this day, I am absolutely steadfast in honoring this rule. Incomplete personal woodworking projects get finished within a reasonable period or get sacrificed to the woodstove or scrap bin. Tools, shop accessories and storage systems are hung on the wall whenever possible, and permanently fixed workbenches, nonfolding sawhorses and certain immobile large power tools are taboo. The end result is an open, easy-to-clean workshop: Each workstation has ample room, the raw materials and components flow easily through the space, and everything needed to produce a product lies close at hand.

The second rule that bubbled up out of the primordial sawdust concerns the production process itself. Simply stated, it is this: *No project will be assembled until there is a place outside the*

shop for it to go. Because assembled components in this business uncannily resemble empty boxes, storing them renders vast amounts of space essentially useless. To minimize this small-shop gridlock, I have developed a production method over the years that places assembly at the very end of the process. Allegiance to this rule simply requires that a project be scheduled for installation immediately after assembly. This doesn't mean that only one project can be processed at a time. In fact, the block production method detailed later in this book actually makes it easy to do several jobs at one time. I've had as many as three projects in flat storage units awaiting assembly. The project that gets built is simply the one that receives site clearance first.

With these two rules now reliefcarved in ebony, get busy and create your perfect shop. This section covers location, utilities and structural considerations of the shop; layout of the major tools and workstations; and the tooling, both manual and power, that you will need to make it in this business.

1 | location and work space

Let's assume we are going to create a perfect shop from scratch. This is the best way to start, especially if you are currently stuck in a compromising shop situation. Besides, after you read this chapter, you may decide to move to a new shop anyway.

Where to Locate

The first issue to consider is whether you want your shop to be at home or a commute away. Part of the answer will arise from taking an honest look at your personal habits. Some people can work effectively at home on a daily basis, whereas others have difficulty putting in a single productive eight-hour day at home over the course of a week. The problem with a home shop is, of course, that the attractions of home life beckon just outside the shop's door.

It is, however, well worth the effort to learn to work productively at home. Overhead is likely to be much lower than for a separate shop, and there is no expense for a commute. Even more important is the coherency that your life can achieve when home and work form a symbiotic relationship. It's part of the old American dream, and part of the gift of being a cabinetmaker that is worth experiencing.

Unfortunately, you may not be able to have a shop at home. Consider a few things before you decide.

Unless your name and reputation are already well established, your shop should be close to the region's job market. If your home is an hour's drive over poor roads to the nearest town, your clients will have to really want to give you their business to justify passing all those other cabinetmakers on their way to your place. Of course, the better your work is and the more competitively you price it, the further they will be willing to drive — but only to a

point. If your home is not on the clients' side of that point, you probably shouldn't have your shop there.

The trucks that will frequent your shop need good physical access. The driveway must neither swallow vehicles and traveling salesmen every time the rain turns it to mud nor be so steep that the strain of climbing it turns trucks' driveshafts into wet spaghetti. The vehicles must also have a place to turn around.

Another important consideration is whether the law allows you to work in your home. Contact your city or regional planning office to find out whether your property is zoned for commercial use. You can also simply go to the town hall and ask to see the zoning map and the list of attendant ordinances. (Also check for any noise restrictions that might affect you.) As a one- or two-person shop, you will be small, but you won't be invisible. If there's a legal problem with your presence, you might eventually find yourself out of a shop.

One final question: How much can you afford to spend for shop space? The rent or mortgage on shop space is a fixed burden that will affect your ability to turn a profit. Unless you are lucky, prepare to pay big money for a good shop location. If your shop is at home, you have a distinct financial advantage, but locating yourself in an area that affords good visibility to an appreciative clientele will contribute greatly to your ability to carry a higher overhead without jeopardizing your profit margin. If you are just getting started, you will

The cabinet shop of John Marckworth is the 999-square-foot basement of his 1920s vintage bungalow. Its about as small as one could go and still maintain sanity!

probably have to accept a lower profit margin to be able to afford a good location, but make sure you at least cover overhead and earn a wage comparable to that earned by journeyman cabinetmakers at local commercial shops. Try not to compromise on the shop if you can help it, or you may find yourself slowly sinking into the sawdust over a number of years.

Size and Space

If it's legal to work there, if the driveway doesn't eat trucks and if your clients don't ask, "What state are you in?" when you give them directions, then you probably have a good location for your shop. It's time to take a close look at the physical plant, such as overall size and floor configuration, placement of doors and windows, availability of utilities and need for interior structural modifications.

A good shop is not necessarily a large shop. In fact, I would rate ease of access and high visibility far ahead of massive floor space. It's been my experience that a shop as small as 675 square feet (a typical two-car garage, see drawing on page 15) can be adequate for a one-person shop. Too much space can actually be detrimental. In a large shop — such as one approaching 1,350 square feet — you would put extra mileage on your boots as you trudge from one workstation to the next. Excess materials can all too easily find their way into a large shop and impede production flow. You also would find yourself heating, lighting and paying for more space than you really need.

The configuration of the space often determines how well the shop will work for cabinetmaking. Ideally, the space should be square or rectangular; L-shaped or joined spaces with access through partitions usually work against efficient production. In my experience, a simple open square can be used far more efficiently than an unusually configured space of twice the square footage.

In addition to the open shop area, it's nice to have a bathroom and perhaps a bit of covered dead storage. A separate office is a necessity. This quiet, dust-free space is the place to make telephone calls; talk to clients; do design and book work; store and use books, portfolios and product samples; have lunch; and change out of your work clothes. If adding an office to the shop is impossible, consider building an enclosed loft in a high-ceilinged shop or sacrificing a 6' × 6' space in the corner of the work area.

This is the massive shop of The Maizefield Company, Seb Eggert's architectural woodwork shop, which produces mostly custom mantels, fireplace surrounds and doors.

Lighting and Electrical Requirements

Be sure to note whether the shop space you're considering receives ample natural light. Lack of natural light is probably not sufficient reason to turn down an otherwise good space, but a shop buried in the woods or surrounded by tall buildings can be gloomy to work in and expensive to illuminate. Ideally, the shop will be exposed to open sky in at least one direction and have windows situated to take advantage of it and located as high as possible on the walls to keep direct sunlight from playing across the workstations. (The ideal is to have most of the windows high on the north side of the building and to have plenty of opaque skylights in the roof.)

Unless your shop has a waterwheel and jack shafts — or you're just in this for fun and aerobic conditioning — you need electricity. (See the wiring diagram for my shop on the next page.) Ideally, look for at least 100-amp service on its own meter to feed separate lighting and socket circuits for major stationary tools so you won't be in the dark when you blow the breaker.

To keep from landing in the hospital, ground all sockets, along with all your metal tool cabinets and tool stands, to the cold-water pipe or a separate grounding rod. Don't depend on the neutral wire in the 220 feeds to act as a ground: A fourth wire is essential to keep you from lighting up like a Christmas tree if a switch or motor should short out. Don't wire the shop without inspection or certification by a licensed electrician.

Make sure the shop has an adequate lighting system. Fluorescent lighting is an excellent main source of light for the central work area; four to six 8'-long double strips provide pervasive, relatively shadow-free light. Because I dislike the sterile, pulsating quality of this light, I mix in steady warm incandescent light, usually a 200- or 300-watt bulb on the ceiling toward each corner of the shop. Some individual workstations throughout the shop, especially the drill press, the band saw and the sharpening/grinding area, also need spot illumination. Put these lights on individual switches so they can remain off except when needed. In all cases, light sources should be located as high in the space as possible to reduce glare.

Heating

Until recently, the only source of energy I ever used for heating my shop was, wouldn't you know it, wood — and I know many other small, custom woodworking shops that use their raw material for heat. For cabinetmakers, kindling is plentiful, and we already know how to remove splinters. In many areas of the country, wood is still a cheaper source of BTUs than any other fuel, and it allows the option of expending your own time and energy to obtain it.

If you choose this tack, be careful. Woodstoves must be properly installed, and each type of stove has a particular combustible-surface offset requirement. Don't forget that the area under the stove must be noncombustible. Exhaust pipes also have offset requirements, and they need insulated fittings where they pass through the structure. Check with your local fire department for information on the proper installation of a woodstove and exhaust system.

Several other precautions are peculiar to woodstoves in woodshops. If a woodshop has too much of one thing, it's wood. Scraps, offcuts and rejected components build up quickly in the midst of production. Constant vigilance to keep this material contained in scrap bins is necessary. A piece of dry wood left leaning on a wall within the combustion zone will catch on fire — it's just a matter of time. If you do not act within 22 seconds of ignition, the fire will spread to the structure. If you do not act within 2 to 3 minutes, you lose your shop.

Be picky about the type of scraps you burn. There is some dispute about the toxicity of released gas, but I would avoid burning glue-laden materials such as particleboard, plywood and, especially, laminated sheet stock. Immerse oily rags in water; do not burn them in the stove.

Two amenities can make the use of woodstoves more efficient. Ceiling-mounted fans can force warm air down to the floor, heating up the shop quickly and evenly. A woodbox, preferably one that can be filled from outside the shop, contains dirt and nasty bugs that can eat wood faster than a cabinetmaker ripping stock without a dust mask. (Note the woodbox built into the crosscut saw table on page 15.)

Plumbing

Running water is a big plus for a woodworking shop. The perfect shop has a bathroom containing a toilet and sink. (Of course, if perfection is elusive, you can get by with a portable toilet.) Aside from the obvious hygienic benefits, soap and water keep dirty hands from marring the finish under stains. Water also serves as a solvent for various finishes and for some sharpening stones. For efficiency, there is nothing like a cold splash of water on your face to keep you alert through hot, dusty production runs.

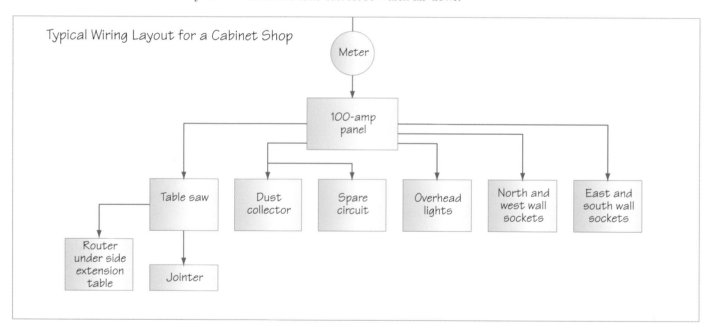

Typical Wiring Layout for a Cabinet Shop

Meter

100-amp panel

Table saw

Router under side extension table

Jointer

Dust collector

Spare circuit

Overhead lights

North and west wall sockets

East and south wall sockets

Whitewash

Make a batch of traditional whitewash by mixing a 50-pound bag of hydrated lime (not garden lime!) with a 10-pound bag of regular table salt and then adding 4 to 5 gallons of skim milk that's past its freshness date (which you can usually get free from your local grocery) until you arrive at a paintlike consistency. If you are going to spray the whitewash, add more milk or some water to thin it.

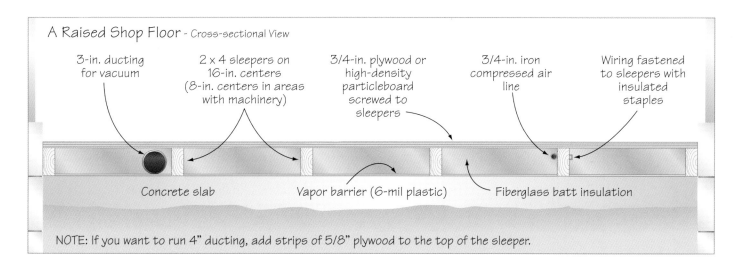

A Raised Shop Floor - Cross-sectional View

3-in. ducting for vacuum

2 x 4 sleepers on 16-in. centers (8-in. centers in areas with machinery)

3/4-in. plywood or high-density particleboard screwed to sleepers

3/4-in. iron compressed air line

Wiring fastened to sleepers with insulated staples

Concrete slab

Vapor barrier (6-mil plastic)

Fiberglass batt insulation

NOTE: If you want to run 4" ducting, add strips of 5/8" plywood to the top of the sleeper.

Structural Modifications

You may also need to add or modify the shop's doors and windows. It's important, for example, to have a large door, preferably a sliding type, located directly ahead of the table saw. As you will see in the discussion of machine layout in chapter two, the major stationary tools should be grouped in as compact a space as possible. A door ahead of the table saw allows this tool group to be positioned to within 8 feet of the shop wall; opening the door provides for ripping and jointing stock longer than 8 feet. If for some reason (a recalcitrant landlord, for example) you can't add a door, perhaps you can install a sliding panel in the wall that is just large enough to pass stock through.

A door for bringing in raw materials and easily removing completed cabinetry is needed. This door should be as large as possible. My shop has large bypass doors on the access face. One slides back when I need room ahead of the saws and jointer; sliding back the other completely opens the wall ahead of the area where I stack cabinets after assembly.

If the shop windows are poorly placed and you are unable to move them, consider covering them with white nylon or canvas to eliminate glare. A good way to brighten the shop's interior is to paint the walls and ceiling with a semigloss white paint. In one shop I rented while on a limited budget, I covered the walls and ceiling

with traditional whitewash—the cheapest, and maybe the best, way to come up with a durable, reflective surface coating. It instantly eliminated grime and dark corners, and it left behind a pleasing, fresh smell. (See the sidebar on page 12 for the formula.)

Another alternative is to nail or screw white-faced building board, sometimes called insulation board, over the existing wall covering or framing. As well as brightening up the shop, the building board will add insulation and significantly lessen noise. An added advantage is that it turns every wall into a bulletin board.

If your shop has a concrete slab for a floor (and most do), consider covering it with something more forgiving. If you try to live with the concrete floor, your legs will ache and fatigue will be your constant afternoon companion. You'll ruin your back and every chisel you own — the chisels will drop edge-first on the floor in obeisance to the laws of physics (and always just after sharpening, in obeisance to the laws of Mr. Murphy). One solution is to cover the concrete with building board and simply lay the sheets snugly again one another. (You can buy the bo with black facing, which is less ex sive than the type with the white ing.) Don't glue the boards down: They'll be difficult to replace, and will have to replace them in the he traffic areas every few years.

A better, albeit more expensive and time-consuming, solution is the floor

construction shown above. Create a raised, "soft" floor by laying down 2×4s on 16" centers over 6-mil vapor barrier. Note that you will have to add ½" spacers to the 2×4s to allow clearance for 4" vacuum ducting. (Alternatively, you can run 3" ducting, though you'll sacrifice some suction power.) Double the framing to 8" centers under the table saw/jointer group to eliminate any give in the floor in this area. Compensate for gaps between the 2×4 sleepers and the slab, caused by hollows in the concrete, by inserting cedar shims. Fasten the sleepers to the concrete slab with black-powder fired ram guns driving cement nails or by throughbolting to lead anchors set into the concrete. Run all the stationary tool wiring, compressed air lines and vacuum ducting along the sides of the sleepers, insert fiberglass batting and screw the ¾" flooring in place. Just think of it: no ‸ng over cords and hoses. To

2 | shop layout

Let's assume you've found a shop space in a suitable location. The shop is 26' x 26' (the size of the ubiquitous two-car garage) and has an additional shed extension running the length of one side that you can convert into an office, bathroom and bit of dead storage. You've brightened up the walls, added building board to the ceilings and installed sufficient lighting. An easy-on-the-feet, built-up floor through which you've run wiring and ducting, lies underfoot. It's time to move in and go to work.

Before you set down any machinery, think about layout: Proper placement of major stationary tools and work surfaces is critical to the creation of a shop that works for you. A good layout will maximize production, reduce operator fatigue and facilitate the smooth flow of materials throughout the shop. Shown at right is the layout that I have found to be nearly ideal for a space of this size. The clustered tool groups in the opposing corners of the shop are readily apparent in the drawing. Note how this maximizes the amount of open floor space. Raw materials enter the shop through the sliding doors on the west wall and get stacked in the north section of the shop on the multipurpose work platform or on lumber racks above the crosscut saw. After processing on the saw/jointer/router group, sized materials get stacked against the east wall. After further processing at the drill press or on the work platform, the components flow to the southern portion of the shop to await final assembly. I've worked with this layout with great success for a number of years. Try it, but feel free to modify it to suit your particular idiosyncrasies.

The Saw/Jointer/Router Group

The grouping of the table saw (with a 3-horsepower plunge router mounted under the side extension table to serve as a shaper), jointer and radial-arm saw comprises the very heart of the cabinet shop. It is worth every effort to ensure that all are securely fixed in proper orientation to each other.

The drawing on page 16 depicts this section of the shop. You can see that the table saw, router and radial-arm saw tables, as well as the wood fence bolted to the jointer fence, are built to the same height. This creates a stock support system that works well: The crosscut saw table doubles as a support for the router; the jointer (with a fixture set on its tables or a strip of wood

attached to the top of the fence) doubles as a support for cutting wide stock on the table saw. This system of tables and supports makes it possible for one person to readily, safely maneuver full sheets of plywood and long lengths of solid stock single-handedly.

As you would expect, an awful lot goes on in this area — it is the most important and most frequently used workstation in the shop. Let's examine some of the details:

Note the drawers built directly under the crosscut saw. These can hold extra blades, push sticks and measurement jigs for the saws; router bits and wrenches for the router; and other miscellaneous accessories associated with this tool group.

The area under the router table houses a wheeled trash bin (see on page 16), which receives cutoffs from both saws. The runoff table ahead of the table saw should be built as large as space permits since the dead space below it serves as a garage for an air compressor and a mobile shop vacuum. Finally, in the same drawing, note the addition of a wood vise to the far left of the crosscut saw table. The vise allows this table to double as a planing bench for hand edging or shaping long stock, thus eliminating the need for a second bench. (Other vise functions are handled by knockdown clamp-support systems.)

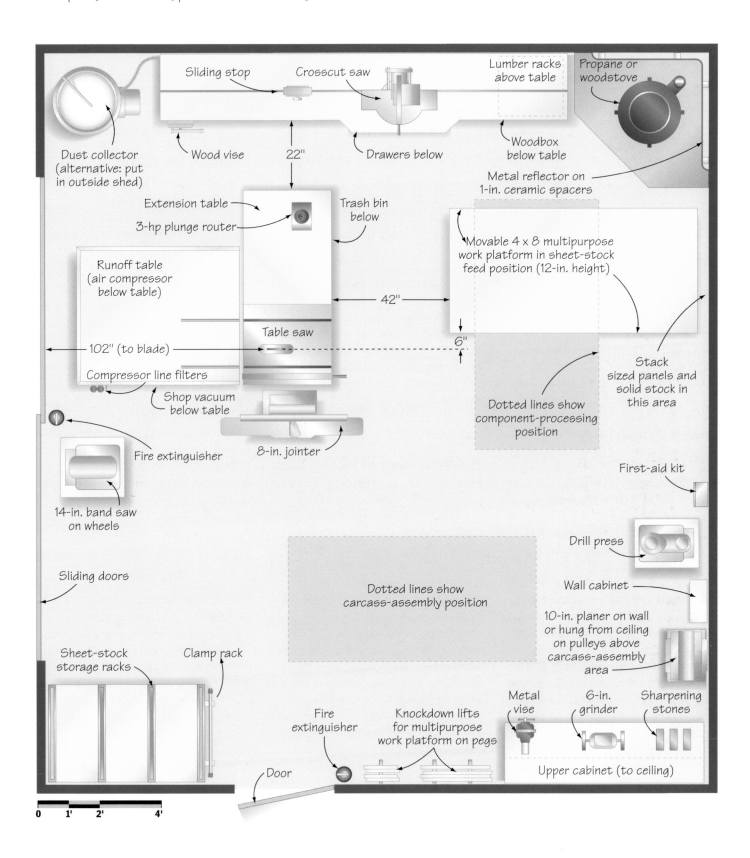

Sliding stop

Crosscut saw

Lumber racks above table

Propane or woodstove

Dust collector (alternative: put in outside shed)

Wood vise

22"

Drawers below

Woodbox below table

Metal reflector on 1-in. ceramic spacers

Extension table

3-hp plunge router

Trash bin below

Movable 4 x 8 multipurpose work platform in sheet-stock feed position (12-in. height)

Runoff table (air compressor below table)

42"

6"

Stack sized panels and solid stock in this area

102" (to blade)

Table saw

Compressor line filters

Shop vacuum below table

Dotted lines show component-processing position

Fire extinguisher

8-in. jointer

First-aid kit

14-in. band saw on wheels

Drill press

Sliding doors

Dotted lines show carcass-assembly position

Wall cabinet

10-in. planer on wall or hung from ceiling on pulleys above carcass-assembly area

Sheet-stock storage racks

Clamp rack

Metal vise

6-in. grinder

Sharpening stones

Fire extinguisher

Knockdown lifts for multipurpose work platform on pegs

Door

Upper cabinet (to ceiling)

0 1' 2' 4'

Shop Dimensions: 22 ft. x 24 ft.

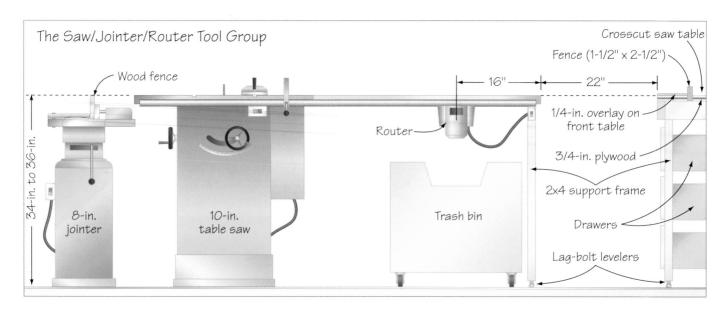

The Saw/Jointer/Router Tool Group

Wood fence

8-in. jointer

10-in. table saw

34-in. to 36-in.

Router

Trash bin

16"

22"

Crosscut saw table

Fence (1-1/2" x 2-1/2")

1/4-in. overlay on front table

3/4-in. plywood

2x4 support frame

Drawers

Lag-bolt levelers

The Drill Press Station

The drill press station is another busy area in the small cabinet shop. I use the drill press to drill holes on door backs to receive European-style cup hinges and to drill the backs of drawer faces for the installation of the attachment hardware. I place this important tool centrally within the production flow: between the area where sized panels and solid stock are stacked and the component-assembly area (see the drawing on page 15). This station also requires a wall cabinet within reach of the quill for storage of drill bits and other related accessories. One further suggestion: Chain the chuck key to some part of the machine. If you don't, you'll waste time looking for the key when it accidentally goes to school in your six-year-old's lunch box someday.

The Grinder/Sharpening Area

Note in the drawing at on page 15 that the grinding/sharpening station is in the corner diagonally opposite the saw/jointer/router group, where it is out of the way yet readily accessible. This is the one area where a little floor space can be sacrificed for a fixed cabinet for storing a host of items, from hardware and sharpening and grinding accessories to hand or power tools not housed in the mobile tool caddy. Mount a wall cabinet for additional tools, fasteners and finishing supplies above the bench. Build it right to the ceiling and

provide access to it with a folding stepladder. In addition to a grinder/sander unit and your sharpening stone or wet-wheel system, this bench can also house a metal vise and perhaps even a small bench-mounted drill press, which comes in handy when the primary unit is tied up in production.

The Placement of Mobile Tools

I make two assumptions here: (1) Your dust collector is immobilized in a corner of the shop (or, even better, in an attached shed) to which you've run ductwork, and (2) you are willing to forego a shaper. (I have found that I can perform nearly all my shaping operations on a 3-hp plunge router mounted under a table. Occasionally I use molding heads on the radial-arm or table saw to shape large patterns, and I have even farmed out volume work to mill shops. In a shop the size of the one we're discussing here, an additional stationary tool creates a real space burden with little net gain in productivity.) These assumptions leave only two major mobile tools to deal with: the band saw and the surface planer.

My band saw has spent a good deal of time roaming around my shop. Its latest location is just ahead of and to the left of the jointer (see the shop map on page 15). So far, its presence here doesn't interfere with the saw/jointer/router group, and I rarely

have to move it to use it (luckily, it's on casters). I think it's finally found a home.

You may be surprised to see the surface planer categorized as a mobile tool. Since the advent of portable surface planers I have discovered that I no longer need the old-time, space-eating, cast-iron monsters. The portable surface planer's light weight allows me to fix it to a 2x4 grid and hang it up, out of the way, on the wall or from the ceiling when it's not in use.

The northwest corner of my old shop housed the major tools — a table saw with a side extension table and an underhanging router, an 8" jointer with a support fence, a radial-arm saw (now replaced by a sliding-arm compound miter saw) and an extension table, a band saw and a dust collector. Note the bin for wood scraps under the table saw's extension table and the work platform in position with sheet stock ready for milling.

The Placement of Work Surfaces and Storage Systems

Since we are woodworkers, we can build ourselves a number of inexpensive fixtures to help us in the workshop. All the construction details for these items are presented in chapter four; for now, let's talk about the proper placement of the fixtures.

Refer again to the drawing on page 15, see the 4' × 8' multipurpose work platform positioned adjacent to the table saw. In this orientation and sitting 12 inches above the floor on a pair of knockdown lifts, it serves as an efficient and back-saving sheet stock feed support. The sequence of photographs on page 18 shows how I can easily maneuver a full sheet of plywood through the table saw by myself. When all the stock has been fed, I place the platform on another pair of lifts at working height (34" for me) and turn it 90° (as indicated by the dotted lines in the shop map on page 15). In this position, the platform becomes my component-processing table. Later, I move the platform back down onto the 12" lifts to create a carcass-assembly area.

Besides the work platform, I have constructed a number of storage racks. As you can see in the map, I built a vertical storage rack for sheet stock in the last unused corner, diagonally opposite the woodstove. If possible, indent this rack into the dead storage area of a shed addition to give you some extra floor space for assembling the cabinets. The lumber rack consumes nearly the entire wall above the crosscut saw table. I use it to store extra stock away from the production flow. Finally, place the clamp rack on a wall as close as possible to the carcass-assembly area.

The southeast corner of the shop contains the drill press, the grinding/sharpening station and storage cabinets. A rolling tool cart is in the foreground.

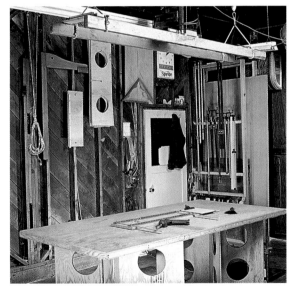

In the southwest corner of my shop, the carcass-assembly platform sits on plywood lifts. The rack in the corner is for stacking surplus sheet stock; it doubles as a clamp rack. The wall stores various equipment out of the way. Note the 10" surface planer hung from the ceiling.

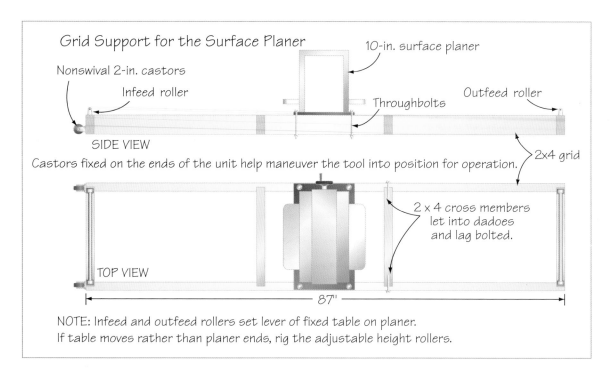

Grid Support for the Surface Planer

Nonswival 2-in. castors

Infeed roller

10-in. surface planer

Outfeed roller

Throughbolts

SIDE VIEW

Castors fixed on the ends of the unit help maneuver the tool into position for operation.

2x4 grid

2 x 4 cross members let into dadoes and lag bolted.

TOP VIEW

87"

NOTE: Infeed and outfeed rollers set lever of fixed table on planer.
If table moves rather than planer ends, rig the adjustable height rollers.

The first step in ripping a full 4' x 8' sheet of plywood is to lift it up from the staging platform by its front edge and draw it up onto the table saw.

Walk to the rear of the sheet and lift it level to the table saw surface. Align the edge against the rip fence.

Push the sheet through the saw. The "shop helpers" roller guides fitted to the rip fence assist in keeping the sheet indexed against the fence. The runoff table supports the sheet as it leaves the saw.

3 | the tools of the trade

Custom cabinetmaking, when practiced on the scale of the independent craftsman, is really not a complex industry. Using the basic workhorses of the average woodshop — plus a decent collection of hand tools and handheld power tools — we can efficiently make high-quality products that reward us with a comfortable livelihood. In this chapter, we'll take a look at the tools that I have found to be essential in achieving success. We'll also talk about adjusting them for maximum efficiency.

To make a decent living at woodworking, you need to own good tools. And, as I'm sure you've noticed, high-quality tools cost good money. For power tools, generally speaking, a more expensive model usually means a more durable and powerful motor, smoother running, and more comfortable to use. The imported Asian machinery, which is cheaper than its American and European counterparts (what's left of them, that is), is something of an exception to this rule.

Good hand tools, no matter where they come from, cost considerably more than inferior versions. However, with some notable exceptions (known especially by aficionados of Japanese toolmakers or cottage industries such as Lie Nielson Tools), even the best tools currently offered for sale are rarely a match for the quality of the professional-grade tools manufactured in the United States prior to World War II. Seek them out before spending the same amount of money, or more, on new tools. (See Appendix 1 for some sources.)

The Table Saw

As a cabinetmaker, you will spend a lot of time cutting plywood and narrowing boards. The table saw will be your constant companion in these endeavors, so you should buy the best one you can afford.

You can purchase a new car, a nice one, for the price of an industrial-grade table saw. However, unless you are gearing up to build strictly European-style laminate cabinetry, you don't need a multibladed, panel-carriage-equipped, computer-driven monster in your shop. What you do need is a solid, relatively powerful, vibration-free saw with a left-tilting arbor saw, at least a 48" rip capacity and an accurately indexed fence system.

You can get by with a 10" contractor's-type saw, as I did for many years. If it's equipped with shop-made fix-

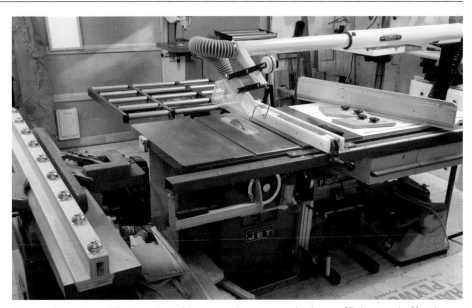

You won't make a living on the table saw unless you make it an efficient and effective tool. The rip fence should slide freely, be set accurately to an index at any length up to at least 48" to the right of the blade and lock down securely. Note the shop-made panic bar mounted beneath the rail, which allows me to shut off the saw with a bump of the hip, and the overarm dust collection system that grabs the dust at the source.

tures, a runoff table (see chapter four) and a precision fence system, you can then upgrade other critical equipment before stepping up from the open-stand contractor's saw.

I highly recommend that you eventually acquire one of the heavier, enclosed-stand units epitomized by the infamous Delta Unisaw. There are many advantages in having a saw of this class. Instead of the contractor's 1-hp or 1½-hp motor, you get a 3-hp motor transferring power over three belts (not just one) to an arbor encased in a heavy, vibration-dampening iron casting. The enclosed motor is not as susceptible to collecting dust. The switch is likely to be magnetic, which can pro-

tect you from shock, and automatically remains shut off after a power break. Finally, if you're accustomed to the controls of lesser saws, you'll really appreciate the beefy cranks that change the height of the blade and the angle of the arbor smoothly and precisely.

Obviously, for consistently accurate, smooth cuts, you should make sure your machine is correctly adjusted according to the owner's manual. (See Appendix 2 for a few other useful places to research fine-tuning of the various machines.) For some of these adjustments, I have found a dial indicator to be invaluable. This machinist's device has plenty of uses, and it's less expensive than a good hand drill.

Using the dial indicator, you can ascertain whether the flange against which the saw's blades are bolted is free of wobble, which is important to know and a check often omitted from saw manufacturers' manuals. With the dial indicator fastened to the table, its arm set against the flange, rotate the arbor by hand and read the amount of variation (or hop-out). It should be less than .001". If it's more, significant vibration may be occurring at the cutting edge of the blade, which prevents really smooth, splinter-free cuts, especially in laminated sheet stock. If you have a problem here, go ahead and sigh deeply; the only solution is to remove the arbor from the machine and have the flange faced at a good machine shop.

If the flange passes inspection, use a combination square to check that the blade runs precisely parallel to the milled grooves in the table surface. Parallelism is essential for smooth cuts when using any jigs, including the rip fence, because the jigs are indexed to the grooves. Use a sequence of three steps to true the blade after unplugging the saw (see box at left). First, hold the bridle of the combination square firmly against the side of the groove closest to the blade. Slide the rule out until it just touches the extreme tip of a marked tooth on the saw blade and lock the bridle in position. Second, rotate the marked tooth to the front of the saw and slide the square forward to meet it. If the plane of the blade and the side of the groove are parallel, the rule will touch the marked tooth just as it did in the first step. If there is deviation, take the third step: Partially loosen the bolts that hold the table surface to the stand and strike a rubber mallet against the side of the table to nullify the deviation. The remaining friction in the bolts prevents the table from moving in large steps. After double-checking the back and front of the blade, retighten the bolts.

Also check the blade angle stop at 90° and 45° using the old pattern-maker's trick of reversing test-cuts to see whether the saw is true at these angles. At a true 90° angle, the re-

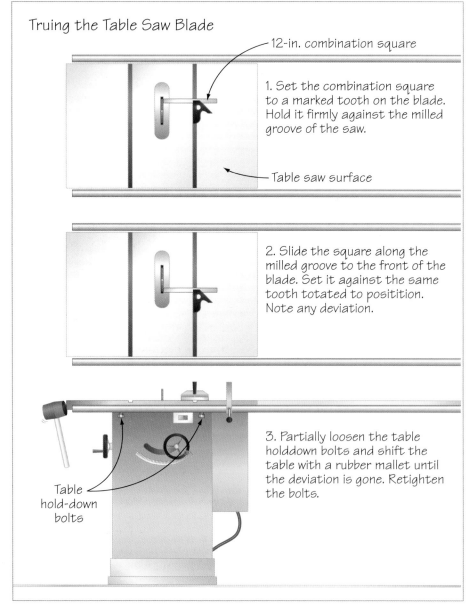

Truing the Table Saw Blade

12-in. combination square

1. Set the combination square to a marked tooth on the blade. Hold it firmly against the milled groove of the saw.

Table saw surface

2. Slide the square along the milled groove to the front of the blade. Set it against the same tooth totated to positition. Note any deviation.

Table hold-down bolts

3. Partially loosen the table holddown bolts and shift the table with a rubber mallet until the deviation is gone. Retighten the bolts.

versed and butted boards will lie flat against a straightedge. At a true 45° angle the boards when reassembled will form a perfect 90° angle. Consult the owner's manual to adjust and tighten down the lock bolts. Finally, make sure the rip fence locks down exactly parallel to the table grooves. Adjust it according to the manufacturer's instructions and lock it securely. (I use a liquid lock washer, available at auto supply stores, to prevent adjustment nuts from loosening with vibration). Make several test-cuts, and adjust the width indicator on the fence.

The accessories you select can add to or sabotage the versatility and safety of your table saw. When it comes to saw blades, you get what you pay for. I recommend that you start with the following small selection of high-quality, carbide-tipped blades: a general-purpose 50-tooth combination blade, a 24-tooth rip blade and a 60-tooth "triple-chip" grind-pattern blade for plywood and laminated sheet stock.

You need a good fence system on your saw; use a system that locks accurately and securely at any distance along its track and moves effortlessly from setting to setting. (See Appendix 1 for information on the variety of fence systems available.) With the fence, I recommend using the shop helpers — those yellow rubber wheels that hold stock firmly against the fence during ripping — made by Western Commercial Products. Since they turn in only one direction, they also prevent kickback. I have found shop helpers to be especially useful when I cut large pieces of sheet stock. I also equip my table saw with a shop-made auxiliary fence to which I can attach a number of other fixtures, including hold-downs and sliding carriages. Complete information on this system — which I call the "universal fence fixture" — can be found in *Jim Tolpin's Table Saw Magic*.

Besides an effective hold-down system, other necessary safety accessories include a functioning blade guard system and a splitter mounted just behind the blade to prevent wood from binding during ripping. Also note in the photo

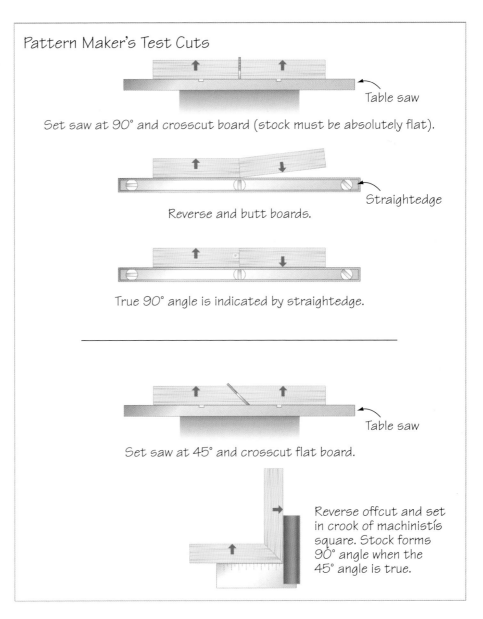

Pattern Maker's Test Cuts

Set saw at 90° and crosscut board (stock must be absolutely flat).

Table saw

Reverse and butt boards.

Straightedge

True 90° angle is indicated by straightedge.

Set saw at 45° and crosscut flat board.

Table saw

Reverse offcut and set in crook of machinist's square. Stock forms 90° angle when the 45° angle is true.

on page 19 the bar mounted below the fence rail on the front of the saw. This shop-made device turns off the saw with a simple bump of the hip. It's fast and certain, and it leaves hands free to control the stock. Finally, I recommend waxing the surface of the saw to prevent the wood from sticking and moving erratically through the blade. All of these accessories work together to prevent an unpleasant surprise — the last thing you want to experience when working with a table saw.

The Crosscut Saw

When I first began woodworking 35 years ago, I immediately became embroiled in the raging controversy of the time: whether the table saw or the radi-

al-arm saw is better for the independent woodworker. The table saw was indisputably the king when it came to ripping stock and handling sheets of plywood, but the radial-arm saw was the champion of versatility and accurate production crosscutting. I solved the controversy for myself by eventually acquiring both and setting them up to complement each other's strengths. I have since replaced the radial-arm saw with the more versatile and easier-to-use sliding compound miter saw.

As the drawing on page 15 shows, in my shop the crosscut saw lives just a step away from the table saw and is set up to do mostly the one task that it does more efficiently than any other tool: accurately crosscut stock at 90°. Once the

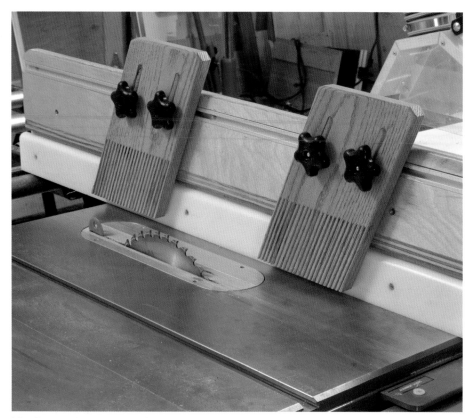

My shop-made accessory fence (which I describe in detail in *Jim Tolpin's Table Saw Magic*) has a variety of guide fixtures and hold-downs.

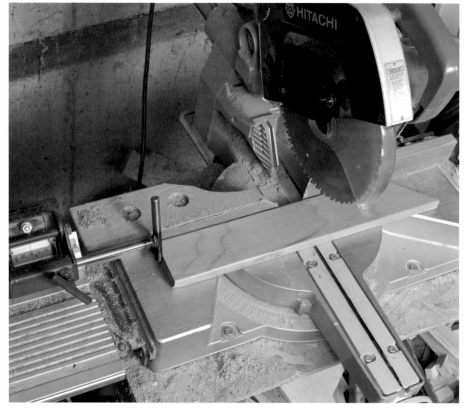

I make most of my rough crosscuts on a miter saw set under the lumber storage racks. An indexed stop makes quick work of setting up the cuts.

tool is precisely adjusted, I rarely change the settings except for the few times I need it to create compound miters. When I occasionally use it to cut a simple angle, I set a wedge against the back fence to bring the stock out to the desired angle rather than move the blade carriage. In general, however, mitering operations are performed not on the crosscut saw but on a sliding jig installed on a table saw.

For consistently smooth, accurate cuts on the crosscut saw, some blade-alignment adjustments may be necessary during initial setup. The owner's manual should explain how to adjust the saw to ensure that the cut will be square relative to the fence and to the table surface. These adjustments are critical to ensure that the front and the back of the blade are perfectly aligned with the travel of the saw along the carriage arm. Thus a horizontal line drawn through the plane of the saw blade will parallel the line produced by the cutting action of the blade. Perfect alignment here is critical to producing accurate, burn-free crosscuts. In my shop only one blade is required for the crosscut saw: a high-quality, 60-tooth ATB (alternate top bevel) carbide crosscut blade.

As shown in the shop layout plan on page 15, the crosscut saw is surrounded by extension tables designed to handle long lengths of solid stock. A dust-collecting duct located just behind the blade removes much of the dust created during a crosscut.

The symbiotic relationship between the crosscut saw and the table saw is consummated by the precise attunement of each machine's indexed fence or stop system. When the rip fence on the table saw cuts a piece of plywood at $24\frac{1}{32}$", the crosscut saw with its indexed stop set at $24\frac{1}{32}$", cuts a length of stock that precisely matches the width of the plywood. Once you trust the relationship between the two machines, you may even feel like you can throw away your tape measure.

The Jointer

The jointer is snuggled in right next to the table saw in my shop and is an integral member of this tool grouping. As a rough edge is created on the table saw, the jointer is right there to straighten and smooth that edge in preparation for the next operation: a second pass through the rip blade, a crosscut at the radial-arm saw or a molding pass on the router. It all happens in this one corner of the shop. A length of hardwood bolted to its fence (or a removable fixture with ball rollers) offers a secondary support to the table saw's surface when large sheets of plywood or long jigs must be maneuvered on the table saw.

You can get by with a 6" jointer, as I did for many years, but if you can afford to acquire an 8" machine, do so. You'll probably wonder how you ever managed on the smaller one. The extra power and table width are perks, but the longer bed that is the real blessing to the one-person shop. Jointing a 12' length of 1×12 single-handedly is no problem with the 8" machine, and you can permanently retire your 24" hand plane (except for fun and exercise).

Although the jointer is a rather simple tool with few moving parts, you need to perform several checks to ensure that it will produce an absolutely flat and straight surface on a piece of wood. First, check the condition of the tables. Use a known straightedge (machine shops sometimes have offcuts with a true edge) to check for flatness and parallelism between the two tables. Detect any twist in the table surfaces with winding sticks. Inserting machinists' brass shims in the ways on which the tables slide, or sometimes simply retightening the gib screws, will usually correct sagging (nonparallel) tables. Major problems of warp, concavity or convexity can be corrected only by resurfacing at a machine shop. Try jointing a number of boards and checking the results before pulling a table — it may not be as bad as it looks.

Adjust the angle of the jointer's fence to 90° against a 6" machinist's square, checking along the length of the

Truing the Jointer Fence to 90

Two jointed boards with marked surface and edge

Jointer set at an angle other than 90

Jointer set at true 90

Reversing indexed surfaces cancels error.

Matching indexed surfaces doubles error.

When edges are jointed 90° to surface and the pieces are butted, one plane results.

fence. If it reads differently (meaning the fence is warped), true the fence to 90° in the vicinity of the blade. If you get more than a few thousandths of an inch variation, however, you may want to either get the fence resurfaced or add a wood surface that you can plane true. Check for a true perpendicular cut by comparing two jointed boards. If any angle other than 90° has been planed on the edges, the faces will not form a straight line (see drawing above). Finally, make sure the blade guard is functioning properly. It should not bind when encountering stock, and it should close quickly behind the board as it passes. Wax the guard where it meets the wood, and keep the pivot well lubricated with a light grease. Also lubricate the table and fence surfaces with wax to avoid erratic feed movement and to reduce drag.

One final note: Save one-third of the blade area exclusively for edging stock, such as particleboard and plywood, that is damaging to the blades. The remaining two-thirds will stay sharp far longer, extending the replacement period significantly.

The Surface Planer

In the early years I owned a handsome, old and heavy (immobile, actually) 16" planer. The 1-hp motor itself was the size of today's typical 10" or 12" planer, and weighed well over 100 pounds — that horse was one obese draft animal. The Red Fox (its brand name) commanded the middle of the shop, and everyone had to work gingerly around it because it obviously wasn't going anywhere. Then one day the light came on in my dust-filled skull, and with the floor groaning a sigh of relief, I booted it out the door and into the arms of an eager boatbuilder. (It actually took more than one boot and one boatbuilder.) In came its replacement: a modern, lightweight (only 50 pounds), 10" portable planer made by Ryobi, which quickly found itself bolted to the 2×4 grid I had prepared for it and hung from the ceiling of the shop.

After years of living with the Red Fox, I was able to go with a light-duty planer because my methodologies were changing. I was no longer buying wood in the rough, I found it far more cost-effective to let the mill surface it to within ¹⁄₁₆" of final dimension before it was delivered to my shop (stock sold this way is designated *S2S*, that is, *surfaced two sides*). By this time, I was also farming out the surfacing of edge-laminated panels to a local mill yard that possessed an accurate, efficient, and, of course, expensive surface sanding machine. Thus I no longer required my surface planer to do much more than the final, uniform dimensioning of stock and the occasional sizing of moldings, trim or spacers.

I recommend that you acquire a lightweight surface planer. The lightweight planers are nearly as fast as much heavier machines. Because of their fast cutter speeds and extremely sharp knives (which are easy to keep sharp with the jigs supplied by the manufacturer), the lightweight planers produce consistently smooth, nearly unblemished surfaces. These machines also appear to be quite durable when used for finish surfacing and light milling, and you can hardly beat the

With the surface planer mounted to a pair of 8'-long 2x4s, I can set it up on sawhorses. Use cross pieces of 2x4 to support the stock to either side. After the surfacing process, I haul the planer back up to the ceiling rafters.

price. Do go the extra mile when buying your planer: Acquire the knife-sharpening jigs and a vacuum chute. If you simply can't live without your version of the Red Fox, I suggest you build it a "fox" house alongside the shop. You'll find something else to do with the vacated floor space, believe me.

The Drill Press

The drill press station is a busy place in the production flow of a typical cabinet job. This is where you produce holes for adjustable drawer-face attachment hardware and for European-style cup hinges. A variety of sanding and grinding attachments add to the versatility of the drill press station.

Whether you select a floor or a bench model drill press (I have both), be sure to securely bolt it in place. The quill should have a speed range of at least 400 rpm to 2,800 rpm, and you should be able to easily shift from one speed to another. A 6" throat capacity, a 3¼" spindle throw and a ½-hp to ¾-hp motor will do the job. I added a surface to the metal table (a 16" × 24" sheet of ¾" plywood works well) to which I installed a fence and stop system. Be sure the table sits exactly perpendicular to

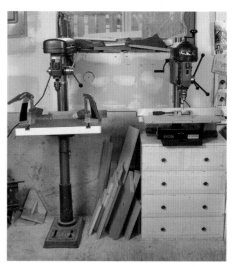

My drill press station now has two machines — a bench unit, featuring a tilting table, that I generally use for finer work and a heavy-duty floor drill press that features an aftermarket table and clamp hold-down system. An old chest of drawers serves as a bit and accessories storage unit.

the travel of the quill when measured from side to side and from front to back of the table. The former is adjusted by simply swiveling the table on its mount; the latter, by adding machinist's shim stock or fine sandpaper between the table and the plywood behind or in front of the quill. (My bench model actually features a front-to-back adjustable table). Finally, a quick-setting, slippage-free stop (for depth regulation) is an absolute necessity.

Like the jointer, the drill press is a rather simple machine: Accurate performance depends on sturdy construction and close tolerances. Your trusty dial indicator can be used to check a number of critical adjustments. Clamp its base to the table (which should be locked down) and swing the indicator's arm against the edge of the chuck. The run-out should be less than .001". If it's more than that, you likely have an inferior drill press. If it looks good so far, insert a trued $\frac{1}{2}$" steel rod (see your local machinist for a loaner) in the chuck. As you rotate the spindle by hand (be sure the drill is unplugged), the dial will read out the amount of run-out. It should be less than .004". If the amount of run-out changes when you reseat the rod, you are probably dealing with an inferior chuck. The fix is to replace it with a better one. If the problem persists, you may need to have the taper in the quill reground at a good machine shop.

The Band Saw
It would be hard for me to live without my old 14" Rockwell band saw, although I probably could get by with a good jigsaw if I had to. Since my band saw lives on wheels and has found an unobtrusive home in my shop (see the shop layout drawing on page 15) it doesn't have to worry about going the way of the Red Fox — the victim of my fanatical quest for unobstructed floor space. In truth, nothing is quite like a band saw for cutting arches in the rails and panels of doors and for introducing nice curves into lintels, aprons and support brackets. I also use the band saw for producing notches in the top of partitions and occasionally for roughing out a variety of hand-finished joints, such as bridles, half-laps and through-tenons.

Unless you need resaw capabilities (perhaps you like to resaw found lumber for unusual door panels), you can get by with a $\frac{3}{4}$-hp saw with a 14"

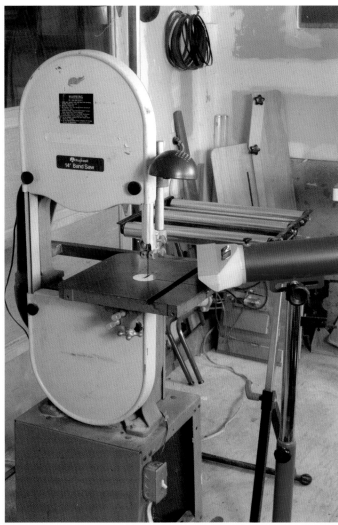

To increase efficiency and safety, my band saw station features a roller outfeed stand, a vacuum pickup stand and a gooseneck light focused on the cutting action.

throat capacity and a 6" height of cut. You might even make do with a 12" saw, since its primary function will be to shape the edges of stock less than 2" thick. The saw should, however, be sturdily built. A good one has two support carriages — one above and one below the table for the blade. A sealed ball bearing on each carriage supports the back of the blade when under pressure, and guide bushings support the sides. You will need to adjust the bearing carriages, guide bushings, tracking and tension according to the owner's manual. (See Appendix 2 to find a source of a good review of band saws and their maintenance and adjustment procedures.) I have added a gooseneck lamp to my band saw for task lighting of the cutting area.

The only blade you will probably need is a $\frac{1}{4}$", 6 tpi, skip-tooth blade of either bimetal (which lasts a long time

and can be highly tensioned for ripping) or standard carbon steel. With either type of blade, relieve the tension when the tool will be idle for a long time. Other maintenance procedures include lubricating the table, cleaning sawdust off the wheels and keeping the motor pulley properly tensioned. Finally, a word about safety: *Never* run the saw with the blade guards and the wheel covers removed. I'll never forget the time the blade broke on an ancient 36" ship's saw. Without a guard in place over the top wheel, the blade — all 18' of it — came slithering out like a snake, and with a bloodcurdling shriek, it chased a bunch of boatbuilders around the shop and out into the rain. They wouldn't come back until the shop's welder fashioned a cage for the wheel strong enough to contain a couple of impassioned gorillas.

The Air Compressor

The uses of an air compressor around a cabinet shop are many and worthwhile. Pressurized air blows chips and sawdust out of joints, tool motors and other hard-to-reach areas, and cleans surfaces for finishing. In addition, the compressor can power a wide variety of finishing, surfacing and drilling tools; it can even blow up the tires on the truck and inflate the kids' pool toys.

The first and foremost use of this tool around the shop, however, is to drive fasteners. There is absolutely no substitute for air-powered nail guns for fastening objects together rapidly, securely and without the fear of splitting out the wood or the need to predrill pilot holes. The guns and the fasteners themselves are relatively expensive (avoid trying to save money by buying inferior brands, because you won't), but few tools in cabinetmaking will pay for themselves faster than an air nailer.

You can find a multitude of guns and fasteners, but you can get by with just two such tools: a finish nailer with a capacity for finish nails up to 2" long, and a brad tacker for shooting $5/8$" to 1" slight-headed brads. With these two guns, you can assemble drawers and other components; apply face frames, moldings, trim and bracing elements; aid in some carcass assemblies; and apply on-site moldings and trim.

Powering these tools, requires at least a $3/4$-hp, single-stage compressor unit with a minimum tank capacity of 4 gallons. (Going with a larger motor and greater storage capacity will allow the machine to cycle less frequently, extending the life of the motor and protecting your ears.) For shooting nails, the compressor should deliver at least 90 pounds per square inch (PSI) at 1.8 cubic feet per minute (cfm) through a regulator. If you intend to use the compressor to spray paint or lacquer, be sure it will deliver 5 cfm to 7 cfm at 30 PSI to 38 PSI; to prevent contamination of the finish materials, install oil and water traps (even if the compressor is an oilless type) at the compressor or somewhere near the end of the feed line.

Maintenance of an air compressor is relatively straightforward: Drain the tank frequently to prevent moisture buildup and subsequent corrosion; periodically check the oil level in the crankcase; keep proper tension on the drive belt (if the machine has one); periodically check the action of the safety valve on the tank; and periodically drain the oil and water filters. For safety, make sure all moving parts are covered by a guard (compressors start on their own without warning), and periodically check the condition of the flexible hoses, especially in proximity of any fittings (spend your money on good hoses). Finally, a word of caution: Keep your skin away from close contact with high-velocity compressed air. The incredible pressure could force the air under your skin into your bloodstream and cause a vapor lock in your heart.

Dust Collection

After more than a decade of eating dust and sliding on shavings, not only would I not go without a dust collection system ever again, I probably couldn't work without one. If I had to do it all over, I would have bought a system the day I bought my first table saw — if anyone had made small-scale dust collectors 35 years ago. (See Appendix 2 to find a source of an extensive review of these systems.)

In a small, one-person shop, nearly any floor model currently on the market can suck away the waste of one machine. The most prolific dust producer is probably the surface planer, which, assuming a short length of ducting, requires about a 400-cfm draw from the collector to keep up. Even small machines with a 1-hp motor are generally

This ceiling-mounted filter — which thoughtfully incorporates a light fixture — is capable of drawing all the air of my 550-square foot shop through its filters in about five minutes! With its regular use, I've noticed a drastic reduction in the amount of dust that settles on surfaces.

rated above this level. Perhaps, however, you've decided to run ductwork through the shop as discussed on page 26. In this case, I recommend at least a 2-hp model with a rating of better than 1,000 cfm to make up for friction loss in the ducting and to allow drawing from more than one source at a time (for example, the jointer and the table saw in a sequential operation). Install tight-fitting gates at each station to avoid vacuum loss, and install switches (or, better yet, remotes) to make activation of the collector convenient.

Be aware of the numerous safety considerations with this tool. If plastic ducting is used, you'll need to run a ground wire around the pipe to eliminate static buildup, which has been known to ignite fine dust. Ground metal ductwork as well. Also check to be sure the impeller on the motor is nonferrous (cast aluminum or plastic). Be sure the dust bags are securely fastened to their attachment points, even if that means adding band clamps — if a blow-off occurs when full capacity is reached, the whole purpose of the system is defeated. Finally, keep anything you might want to see again away from the inlets to the system, such as small lengths of molding, fastenings, router bits and smallish pets.

To rid the ambient air of fine dust (i.e., the "fog" of woodworking), install a ceiling-mounted filter that draws the air in and scrubs it clean before blowing it back into the shop. The unit I have installed exchanges the air in my shop about eight times in an hour. With regular use, I've noticed that the horizontal surfaces throughout my shop (and I would guess the same is true of my lungs) stay much freer of fine dust.

The other weapon in my war against dust is an updated version of the old shop vacuum. I use a trigger-activated model into which I plug both the power cord and a hose from my biscuit joiners, orbital sanders and routers. When I turn on the tool, the vacuum comes on and grabs the dust right at the source.

I've placed my 2-hp dust collector in a shed extension to my shop. This welcome move not only freed up floor space but also reduced the amount of noise and fine dust.

Hand Tools

It's been said that the tools of man are but an extension of his wish to manipulate the world around him. I sense, then, that using hand tools, especially those driven by our muscles, come closest to expressing the true nature of our desires. Unfortunately, we feel the need to have lots of tools. Try as we may, we are condemned to the feeling that we do not own the complete set.

It's not really a problem (depending on whom you talk to); you just have to find or build places to put away what you have.

The tables on page 28 list the tools, grouped by power source, that I feel are essential to the efficient construction of cabinetry and casework furniture. (You can find these tools at any of the mail-order houses listed in Appendix 1.)

27

Power Hand Tools

BELT SANDER: For hand-surfacing panels, face frames, etc., 3" x 21" or 3" x 24" is adequate; 4" width is better. Use the dust bag attachment.

ORBITAL SANDERS: One with half-sheet capacity and one with quarter-sheet capacity. I replace stock bases with pads manufactured by 3M for their Stikit sandpaper rolls (see Appendix 1), the only way to go for hand sanding surfaces. They are fast and leave only a minimum of swirl marks. I use a 6" pad size for larger surfaces such as panels and a 5" size for frames. The ideal setup is to connect these sanders to a trigger-activated shop vacuum. Holes in the paper match the holes in the disc, allowing the suction to carry away nearly all the dust.

SLIDING COMPOUND MITER SAW: Great for on-site installation of trim and molding stock. Can be used in place of the radial-arm saw. Sliding fixtures on the table saw mostly do the work of this saw in the shop.

CIRCULAR SAW: For occasional rough-cutting of stock to length, miscellaneous shop repair and construction, and inside cuts on sheet stock; $7\frac{1}{4}$" capacity is adequate.

JIGSAW: Buy a good one. Look for adjustable reciprocating action and variable speed; a tilting base is a plus. Don't leave the shop on installation day without one.

LAMINATE TRIMMER: For laminate installations, breaking edges on wood, producing small molding details.

PLUNGE ROUTER: One of mine is a 3 hp and is permanently mounted under the table saw's side extension table. I have smaller ones for freehand use. Look for $\frac{1}{2}$" collet capacity, positive locking mechanism, comfortable grips.

PNEUMATIC BRAD TACKER: For assembling drawers and other components, attaching solid edge trim and applying various smaller moldings. Brad capacity should be $\frac{5}{8}$" to 1". Buy a good one.

PNEUMATIC NAILERS AND STAPLERS: For attaching face frames, backs, larger trim, molding stock. Nail capacity should be 1" to 2". Better brands are more reliable.

POWER SCREWDRIVER: Even a cheap one will make you glad you never have to drive another small hardware screw by hand.

SPLINE-BISCUIT CUTTER: The tool of choice for quickly creating accurate, strong joints in carcass components and solid-wood frames. Cheaper models are adequate.

POCKET-HOLE FIXTURE: My tool of choice for creating the screw countersink "pockets" that allow you to use screws to clamp components together. I use pocket-hole screws for face-frame joints as well as for attaching the frame to the case itself.

VARIABLE-SPEED DRILLS: Buy at least two, and make one a 9.6V (minimum) cordless. Don't skimp on quality or you'll end up buying replacements. Look for $\frac{3}{8}$" capacity, a reverse function, smooth speed transitions.

Manual Hand Tools

These tools, stored in a mobile tool caddy, accompany me to each workstation in the shop.

MARKING UTENSILS: Pencils (no. $2\frac{1}{2}$) and sharpener, chalk, pens, marking knife, awl, mortise and marking gauges.

LAYOUT DEVICES: Tape measure ($\frac{3}{4}$" x 16') and squares (24", 12" and 6" combination; 6" machinist's). Architect's scale, bevel gauge, protractor, dividers, calculator, trammel points, inside/outside calipers, foot/inch calculator.

CUTTING TOOLS: Set of cabinetmaker's beveled-edge chisels ($\frac{1}{4}$" to 2"), $1\frac{1}{2}$" Japanese push chisel. Planes: block, finger, rabbet, no. 4, no. $4\frac{1}{2}$ smooth. Saws (all Japanese): dovetail, combination rip/crosscut, panel, keyhole. Utility knives.

FINISHING TOOLS: Set of cabinet scrapers, adjustable angle scraper holder, set of hand files, glue scrapers in several shapes.

FASTENING AIDS AND DEVICES: Set of Phillips, slotted- and square-head screwdrivers. Set of high-speed drill bits. Hammers: 13-ounce claw hammer, tack hammer, rubber and/or shot-filled mallet. Brad pusher, nail sets, punches. Set of Fuller countersink bits.

GRASPING DEVICES: Pliers with wire cutters, vise grips, end snippers, set of hex wrenches, small set of open-end wrenches, nail-pulling lever, removers for tacks and staples.

I keep tools elsewhere in the shop — hanging on walls or stored in drawers below the sharpening station bench. Specific delineation of the hordes of router bits, specialized drill bits and other such accessories is excluded — you'll meet them when we call for their help in section two of this book.

CLAMPS: Four sets each of 2', 3' and 4' pipe, Bessey K-body and/or bar clamps; numerous extra lengths of pipe. One dozen 6" C-clamps. Two 36" back-to-back bench clamps (made by Griset Industries; see Appendix 1). Four cam-activated guitar clamps. Several sizes of spring clamps, deep-throat clamps, band clamps.

LEVELS: Reservoir-type water level (for establishing reference line during installations), 30" and 78" bubble levels, torpedo level. I recently upgraded to a laser level that shoots a vertical line as well as a horizontal line.

MISCELLANEOUS: Glue applicators, roller for laying down laminates, electronic stud finder, putty knives in various shapes, spokeshaves, stiff-bristle file cleaner, layout ruler for 32mm-system machine setups, dial indicator, time clock, fire extinguishers and a radio tuned to your favorite station.

The Sharpening Station

The bench located in the sharpening/grinding area of my shop contains all the equipment necessary to handle all my sharpening needs, except sharpening carbide-tipped circular saw blades and router bits. A 6", $\frac{1}{2}$-hp grinder sits next to my primary sharpening system: a Tormek waterwheel. A collection of waterstones sits in a tub of water in the utility sink. To use them, I simply lift them out of the tub and set them on a piece of plywood that I've fixed on top of the sink. Stored in the top drawer of the cabinet below are various sharpening jigs and accessories, a high-speed Dremel grinder-polisher and a small assortment of burnishing tools.

The shaft on one end of the 6" grinder is fitted with a $\frac{3}{4}$" × 6", 100-grit friable abrasive wheel. This type of wheel runs cooler than standard, non-friable wheels and is used for the initial grinding of the primary bevels of drill bits, plane irons, chisels and other edge tools. I do not, however, develop the finished, razor-sharp edge on plane irons and chisels on the grinder. Instead, I move the blades over to the Tormek waterwheel, where I can more easily control the speed of the cut and completely avoid overheating the edge. The Tormek system includes a variety of holding fixtures to hold everything from hand plane irons to chisels to surface planer blades at the correct sharpening angle. To reflatten the water wheel, I regularly hold a diamond-encrusted sharpening plate against the turning wheel for several seconds.

You can create razor-sharp edges by rubbing them on flat waterstones. To reduce the time and effort, I generally create a secondary bevel (or microbevel) on the cutting edge; then I don't have to hone the entire length of the bevel. I use a honing guide to fix the blade at the microbevel angle as I rub it over a sequence of Japanese waterstones of 800, 1500 and 6000 grit. One of the beauties of waterstones is that they are lubricated with (surprise!) water, avoiding the contagion of oil that can seriously damage many wood finishes. Perhaps an even greater benefit of waterstones over oilstones is the ability to reflatten waterstones by simply rubbing them over a hard, flat surface. For this purpose, you can use a $\frac{1}{2}$"-thick sheet of plate glass onto which you sprinkle some fine silicon carbide powder (400 grit or higher). These days, I use a diamond sharpening plate. In any case, the flattening of the stones is critical to produce flat — and therefore perfectly sharp — cutting edges.

I occasionally fit planer blades from the jointer or surfacer into specialized jigs made for this purpose and hone them over the waterstones or the Tormek waterwheel. Usually, however, to save time I send these blades out with the table saw blades for sharpening at a commercial shop and install the sharp second set I keep on hand.

The metal vise mounted on the bench holds specialized drill bits (such as Forstner bits), plug cutters and high-speed steel router bits in position for sharpening. I use either the Dremel tool, fitted with a grinding or buffing wheel, or a set of small tapered files to bring these bits up to par. The vise also holds cabinet scrapers securely while creating the cutting burr with a burnisher.

My sharpening station is comprised of two grinders. One is fitted with a white grinding wheel for reshaping bevels, the other is a Tormek.

Here I'm flattening the back of a chisel on a diamond stone. Notice that I'm using a short length of 1x2 to evenly distribute the pressure. I hone on the diamond stone until the entire back is flat, then I switch to a 6,000-grit waterstone and hone until the metal becomes a mirror.

4 | shop-built fixtures

In this chapter, we will discuss a variety of shop-made fixtures that will help you use your shop more efficiently. Runoff and extension tables for the table saw and crosscut saw fully support the materials being processed, eliminating the need for a helper (even for full sheets of $3/4$"-thick plywood). The table saw's side extension table also supports a 3-hp plunge router, adding a shaping function to this workstation. The multipurpose, multilevel work platform, which rests on knock-down lifts, is a feed platform for sheet stock, a work surface for component processing and a platform for carcass assembly. A variety of storage fixtures increase the chances that certain tools and materials get put away. Finally, three mobile caddies (I call them "stooges") participate in the cabinetmaking process: Moe carries the manual hand tools listed in the table on page 28, Larry shoulders raw materials and component parts and Curly is a trash bin on wheels.

Table Saw Runoff and Side Extension Tables

The runoff and side extension tables provide flat, slippery surfaces that sit level to the plane of the table saw table. The side extension table completely fills the open space between the rip fence guide rails extending to the right of the saw. The runoff table sits ahead of the saw and can be built as large as space permits. Both tables are constructed of laminate-covered $3/4$"-thick

sheet stock screwed to a softwood framework and supported on 2×4 legs that feature a built-in leveling system.

The first step in constructing the tables is to determine their dimensions. The side extension table should precisely fit the space created between the guide rails, while the runoff table should be sized so that it doesn't interfere with the operation of the jointer (or sliding table, if you have one) and to allow a person to pass between it

and the door ahead of the saw. When cutting the sheet stock to size, remember to allow for the $3/4$" × $1\frac{1}{2}$" hardwood edge cap shown in the drawing on page 31. Laminate the sheet stock on both sides to prevent uneven absorption of moisture and subsequent warpage. Select a neutral color with a matte finish to reduce eyestrain and glare (I chose battleship gray).

Build the support framework from $3/4$" × $3\frac{1}{2}$" pine or alder; use spline-bis-

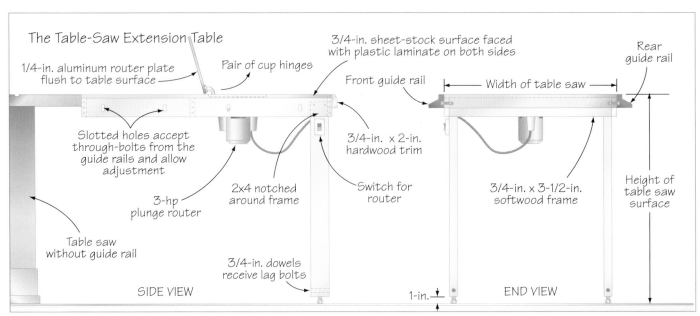

The Table-Saw Extension Table

1/4-in. aluminum router plate flush to table surface

Pair of cup hinges

3/4-in. sheet-stock surface faced with plastic laminate on both sides

Rear guide rail

Front guide rail

Width of table saw

Slotted holes accept through-bolts from the guide rails and allow adjustment

3-hp plunge router

2x4 notched around frame

3/4-in. x 2-in. hardwood trim

Switch for router

3/4-in. x 3-1/2-in. softwood frame

Height of table saw surface

Table saw without guide rail

3/4-in. dowels receive lag bolts

SIDE VIEW

1-in.

END VIEW

cuit joints, glue and screws to fasten the components together. Fasten the sheet surface to the softwood framing from below, using pocket screws or figure-8 fasteners. Construct the legs from 2×4s cut to length, notch them around the frames and screw them in place. Insert ¾" dowels across the 2×4s near the boards' lower ends. These receive the threads of lag bolts, which act as precision levelers for adjusting the surfaces flush to the table-saw surface.

Secure the extension table to the table saw by bolting the guide rails to the extension table's framework. Make the shank holes in the frame vertically elongated slots so you can adjust the height of the table. Note that the ¼" aluminum plate to which the 3-hp plunge router is attached is flush to the surface and hinged from below with cup hinges to allow access to the router from above. (See Appendix 1 for sources of router plates.) Also note the location of the switched outlet for the plunge router.

The runoff table stands independently. Tie it to the table saw by screwing it directly to the guide rail; if this isn't possible, bend two ⅛" steel straps to span the gap between the frame of the runoff table and the metal shroud of the saw. The grooves cut in the surface of the runoff table allow the unobstructed use of sliding jigs and the miter gauge.

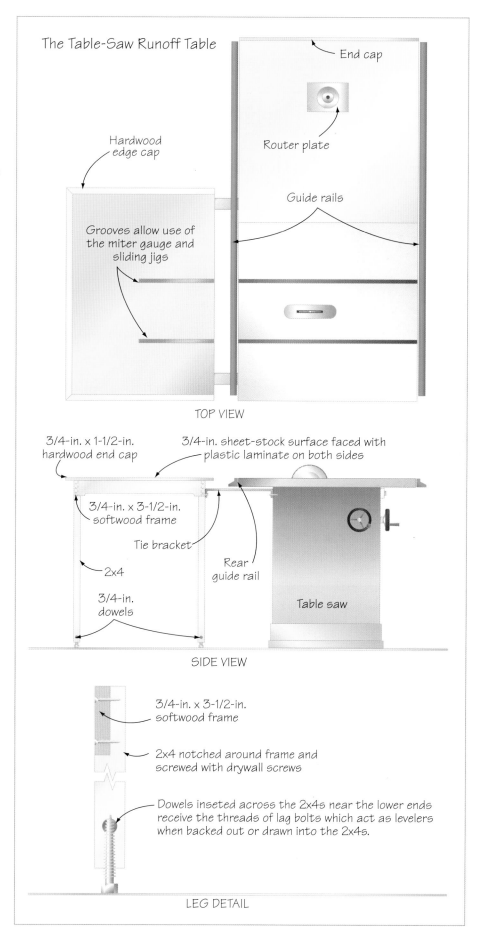

The Table-Saw Runoff Table

End cap

Hardwood edge cap

Router plate

Guide rails

Grooves allow use of the miter gauge and sliding jigs

TOP VIEW

3/4-in. x 1-1/2-in. hardwood end cap

3/4-in. sheet-stock surface faced with plastic laminate on both sides

3/4-in. x 3-1/2-in. softwood frame

Tie bracket

Rear guide rail

2x4

Table saw

3/4-in. dowels

SIDE VIEW

3/4-in. x 3-1/2-in. softwood frame

2x4 notched around frame and screwed with drywall screws

Dowels inseted across the 2x4s near the lower ends receive the threads of lag bolts which act as levelers when backed out or drawn into the 2x4s.

LEG DETAIL

Crosscut Saw Extension Table

The crosscut saw's extension table is composed of three separate units tied together with a full-length fence. The fence acts as a backstop for the stock being crosscut and carries a sliding stop that indexes the length of cut. The central unit supports the saw, while the side units support the material level with the saw. Note that these tables are built to the same height as the table saw's primary and extension tables. Build the side units from 2×4s and make them as long as space permits — I recommend at least 8' to the left of the blade and 6' to the right. Unlike the table saw's runoff and extension tables, the surface of the crosscut saw's table is not laminated; use $3/4$" sheet stock faced with $1/4$"-thick vinyl board. This allows you to create a groove to capture sawdust between the table and the fence and to easily replace the area that is constantly scored by the saw's blade. (I simply stick down a 2"-wide section of the $1/4$" vinyl stock with double-sided carpet tape.)

Do not begin construction of this table until you've built and leveled the table saw's runoff and extension tables. Extend a level line from the table saw surface to the wall against which the radial-arm saw will rest. Measure down 1" from this line (to account for the $3/4$" sheet stock table with its $1/4$" vinyl fac-ing) and extend a level line along the full length of the wall.

Start construction with the central unit, which will support the saw itself. To find the height of this unit (composed of a 2×4 framework fastened to the wall at the back and supported in front by legs with adjustable feet), measure the height of your crosscut saw from its base to its table surface and subtract this measurement from the upper reference line on the wall. Mark a level line on the wall at this height and build the central unit to meet it. Now build the framework of the two side units to the height of the reference line drawn 1" below the first reference line you made (the one that matches the height of the table saw) and securely attach the frame to the wall.

Screw the back table surface down to the framework, and construct the full-length fence. Build the $1^1/2$"-wide by $2^1/4$"-high fence by laminating $3/4$" stock, overlapping lengths and gluing and screwing the assembly together (remove any screws in the way of the saw blade after the glue has dried). Build the fence on the table framework, which, having been leveled, should be perfectly flat.

Secure the fence to the table with 3" drywall screws, adjusting shims in between the fence and the back table surface as necessary to produce a perfectly straight fence face. (Any curvature in the fence will sabotage the 90° crosscuts you aim to produce.) Begin by placing an untapered $1/4$" shim near either side of the blade, then work your way out toward each end of the fence, placing and adjusting tapered shims on 16" centers. Continue adjusting the shims until a long straightedge indicates that the face of the fence is perfectly straight. Then screw through the fence and the backing shims into the backing table. Now you're ready to lay the $3/4$" sheet-stock front table on the support framing and screw it in place. Finally, install the vinyl sheeting, leaving a $1/8$" groove between the sheet and the face of the fence to allow sawdust to get out of the way of the stock — which in turn assures that the stock will sit tightly against the fence.

Next install the right-to-left-reading tape (see Appendix 1 for sources). Measure out 12" from the saw blade to the left along the face of the fence, make a mark, then square it up and over the fence with a combination square. Use this line to index the 12" mark on the tape. Carefully begin sticking down the tape, rolling it out first to the right, then all the way to the left. Don't worry if you come out a little off the mark: The sliding stop has ample adjustment to fine-tune the setting during actual test-cuts.

The Crosscut Saw Extension Table

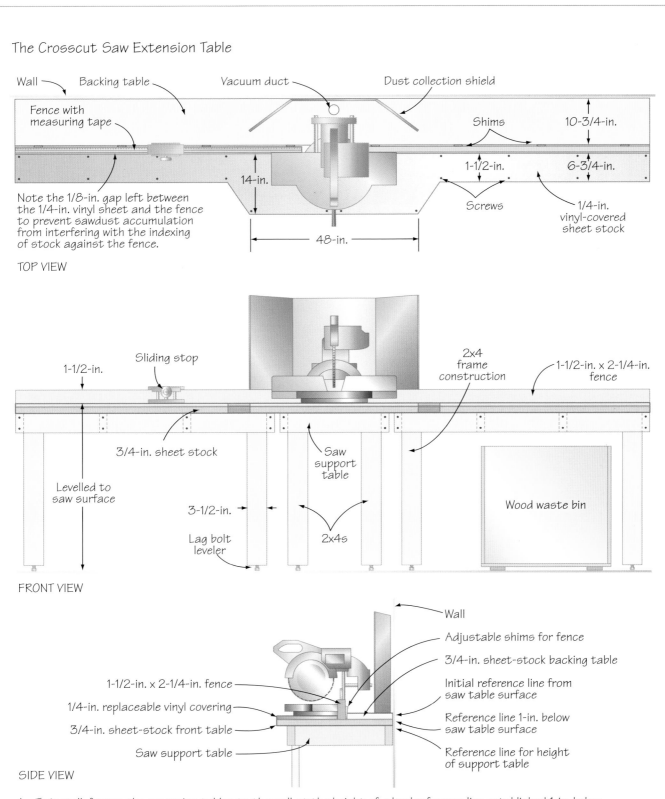

TOP VIEW

Wall

Backing table

Vacuum duct

Dust collection shield

Fence with measuring tape

Shims

10-3/4-in.

1-1/2-in.

6-3/4-in.

Note the 1/8-in. gap left between the 1/4-in. vinyl sheet and the fence to prevent sawdust accumulation from interfering with the indexing of stock against the fence.

Screws

1/4-in. vinyl-covered sheet stock

14-in.

48-in.

FRONT VIEW

1-1/2-in.

Sliding stop

2x4 frame construction

1-1/2-in. x 2-1/4-in. fence

3/4-in. sheet stock

Saw support table

Levelled to saw surface

Wood waste bin

3-1/2-in.

Lag bolt leveler

2x4s

SIDE VIEW

Wall

Adjustable shims for fence

3/4-in. sheet-stock backing table

1-1/2-in. x 2-1/4-in. fence

Initial reference line from saw table surface

1/4-in. replaceable vinyl covering

3/4-in. sheet-stock front table

Reference line 1-in. below saw table surface

Saw support table

Reference line for height of support table

1. To install, fasten the extension tables to the wall at the height of a level reference line established 1-in. below the saw table surface.
2. Level the table frame by adjusting the lag bolts in the base of the 2x4 leg supports.
3. Screw the 3/4-in. sheet-stock backing table in place and fasten the full-length fence to it through the shims.
4. Install the front table, overlay the 1/4-in. vinyl-coated sheet and screw it in place.

The Multipurpose Work Platform

The 4' × 8' work platform serves as a feed platform for sheet stock when it is adjacent to the table saw. When relocated and raised, it acts as a component-assembly table. Lowered back down, it becomes a carcass-assembly platform. Two pairs of simple knockdown lifts hold the platform at these two heights.

The platform itself has a torsion box construction. It consists of a framework of $\frac{3}{4}$" × $1\frac{1}{2}$" softwood sandwiched between sheets of plywood and glued and screwed to each side. Seven-ply, void-free, $\frac{1}{2}$"-thick hardwood plywood is ideal for the top surface; $\frac{3}{16}$" plywood is adequate for the bottom. The result is a relatively lightweight but immensely strong warp-resistant surface.

I borrowed the idea for the knockdown lifts from laminate installers, who often deal with large sheets of this unwieldy material. Construct the lifts from almost any grade of $\frac{3}{4}$"-thick plywood. Go the extra mile: Apply hardwood edging to the perimeter to reduce splinters and increase durability. These lifts also work without the platform to hold various components during processing and finishing operations. You can build more of these supports at a variety of heights to serve additional support functions as the need arises. Color-code the pairs to avoid mis-matching.

Storage Systems

It's important to have ample storage racks and cabinets in a workshop. It's absolutely critical to efficiency (and to mental health!) to make sure tools and materials have a place to be out of the way when they are not needed and to be found when they are. Storage systems are key in the quest to gain as much uncluttered floor space as possible.

LUMBER RACK: Make a lumber rack from 2×4 uprights and some simple $\frac{3}{4}$"-thick plywood brackets. (If the stored lumber will be at least 22" wide, double the number of brackets to support the additional weight.) Mark each upright in the same position (about 4' from the bottom end); when installing, align these marks with a level chalk line snapped along the wall. Use lag bolts to

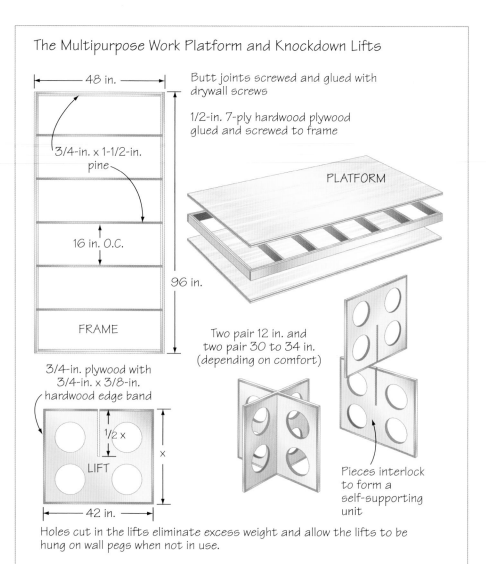

The Multipurpose Work Platform and Knockdown Lifts

48 in.

3/4-in. × 1-1/2-in. pine

16 in. O.C.

96 in.

FRAME

Butt joints screwed and glued with drywall screws

1/2-in. 7-ply hardwood plywood glued and screwed to frame

PLATFORM

3/4-in. plywood with 3/4-in. × 3/8-in. hardwood edge band

1/2 x

LIFT

x

42 in.

Two pair 12 in. and two pair 30 to 34 in. (depending on comfort)

Pieces interlock to form a self-supporting unit

Holes cut in the lifts eliminate excess weight and allow the lifts to be hung on wall pegs when not in use.

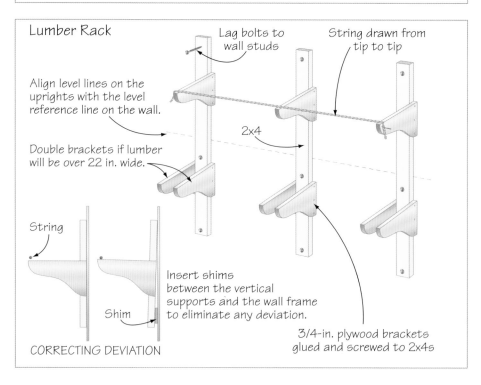

Lumber Rack

Lag bolts to wall studs

String drawn from tip to tip

Align level lines on the uprights with the level reference line on the wall.

2x4

Double brackets if lumber will be over 22 in. wide.

String

Shim

Insert shims between the vertical supports and the wall frame to eliminate any deviation.

CORRECTING DEVIATION

3/4-in. plywood brackets glued and screwed to 2x4s

fasten the uprights to the wall studs, installing the end uprights first; be sure to plumb the brackets out from the wall as necessary. Plumb the intermediate uprights by aligning their tips with a string pulled taut from the tip of one end bracket to the other.

CLAMP RACK: Build this device from 2×4s and a closet pole, and make it as wide as necessary to contain your collection of pipe and bar clamps. The closet pole should hold as many C-clamps as you plan to own. Bolt the rack to the wall studs through nailers dadoed into the uprights.

SHEET STOCK BINS: This rack holds sheet stock between 2×3 grids (2×4s are overkill and take up space) nailed to the floor and ceiling of the shop. Install horizontal plywood strips and a plywood floor to help you slide the panels in and out. Build the rack as tall as the ceiling height allows.

STORAGE CABINETS: The cabinet below the sharpening bench could be the only full-scale example of your work on display when a prospective client walks into your shop, so build it with that in mind. I find cabinets that are chock-full of drawers to be far more useful than those that simply provide enclosed storage space. Some of the drawers can be quite large, providing storage for an assortment of handheld power tools and the opportunity to show off slick, heavy-duty, full-extension drawer slides. Since Murphy's Law dictates that the object of desire will always be in the back corner of any drawer, consider incorporating full-extension slides in the other drawers as well. Protect the cabinet with a water-resistant finish, such as lacquer or a polyurethane varnish; the presence of the water-stones above will assure a steady trickle of liquid onto the cabinet face below.

The cabinet above the bench can be a standard, adjustable-shelf upper. Build it right up to the ceiling, and fit it with plenty of shelves — you will eventually use every inch of them. Build a nice set of doors for this cabinet to keep out dust and to give you and your walk-ins something pleasant to view.

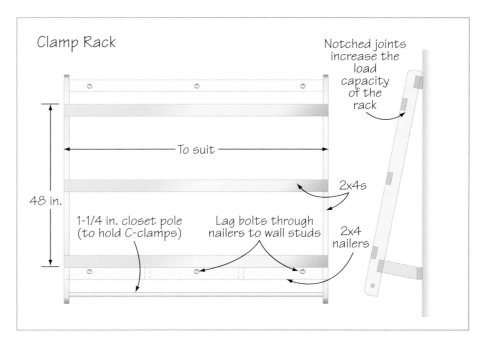

Clamp Rack

Notched joints increase the load capacity of the rack

To suit

48 in.

1-1/4 in. closet pole (to hold C-clamps)

Lag bolts through nailers to wall studs

2x4s

2x4 nailers

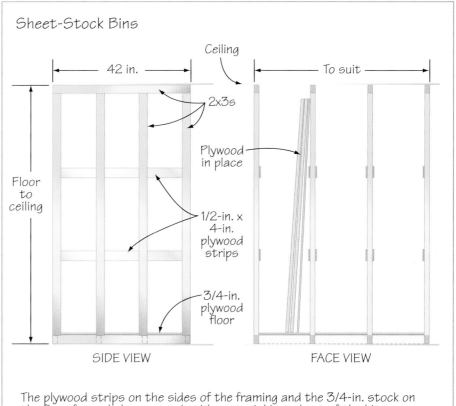

Sheet-Stock Bins

Ceiling

42 in.

To suit

2x3s

Plywood in place

Floor to ceiling

1/2-in. x 4-in. plywood strips

3/4-in. plywood floor

SIDE VIEW

FACE VIEW

The plywood strips on the sides of the framing and the 3/4-in. stock on the floor frame help ease and guide material in and out of the bins.

The Three "Stooges"

Wherever you go and whatever you do in the shop, there's an excellent chance that Moe, your mobile tool caddy, will be right there by your side. Like the sharpening bench's lower cabinet, Moe will be most useful if all the storage is provided by drawers riding on full-extension slides. Build multiple divisions within the drawers so you can sort loose items.

Construct Moe stoutly from ¾" sheet stock and give it four quality, full-swivel 2½"-diameter wheels. Cutouts in the top overhangs provide convenient hand grips. Bins contain an assortment of fasteners; pegs hold additional tools such as hand saws and squares. Careful workmanship will allow this tool cart to withstand years of use, and a durable finish will keep Moe looking good.

Larry, the materials "stooge," is the muscle of the trio. Larry should be able to carry an incredible amount of raw materials and components from one production station to the next. To do the job well, however, Larry must be carefully and sturdily built. Since Larry's structure is an open framework, obtain dimensional stability by using relatively large, tightfitting and thoroughly secured joinery, as shown in the drawing on page 37. Construct the upper platform and the lower shelf frames from ¾" × 4" board stock; join them with glued and screwed spline biscuit joints. Throughbolt the completed frames to the L-shaped legs and install the ½" plywood top surface. The small strips at each end of the top platform keep material in place as Larry grooves from one scene to the next. Since grooving is groovier with larger wheels, especially for heavier fellows, give Larry 3" full-swivel casters.

Last is Curly, the perambulating trash bin. Construct Curly from ¾" plywood fastened around a 2×4 base frame riding on four 2½" full-swivel casters. (Because this rather homely "stooge" will spend a lot of time hiding under the table saw's side extension table, you can build it from any scrap plywood.) Screw the box structure together, and use support blocking in the corners. Determine the height of the bin based on the distance between the floor and the plunge router hanging below the table.

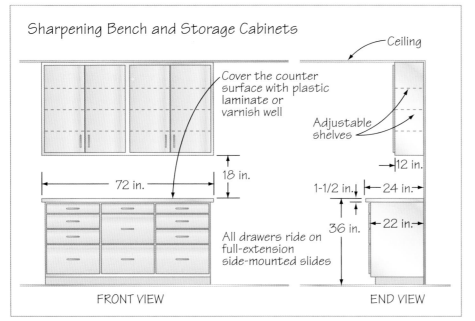

Sharpening Bench and Storage Cabinets

Ceiling

Cover the counter surface with plastic laminate or varnish well

Adjustable shelves

72 in.

18 in.

12 in.

1-1/2 in.

24 in.

36 in.

22 in.

All drawers ride on full-extension side-mounted slides

FRONT VIEW

END VIEW

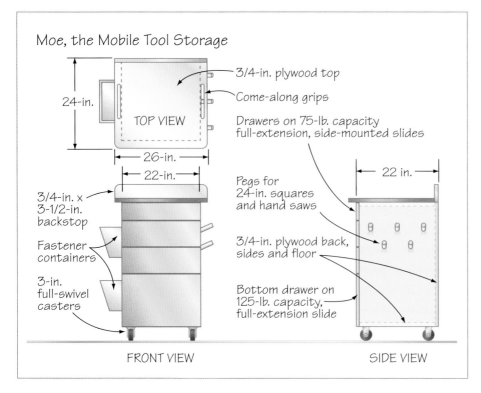

Moe, the Mobile Tool Storage

24-in.

TOP VIEW

3/4-in. plywood top

Come-along grips

Drawers on 75-lb. capacity full-extension, side-mounted slides

26-in.

22-in.

3/4-in. × 3-1/2-in. backstop

Pegs for 24-in. squares and hand saws

22 in.

Fastener containers

3/4-in. plywood back, sides and floor

3-in. full-swivel casters

Bottom drawer on 125-lb. capacity, full-extension slide

FRONT VIEW

SIDE VIEW

A family portrait (from left to right) Larry, the materials cart; Moe, the rolling tool caddy; and Curly, the mobile trash bin.

Larry, the Materials Storage

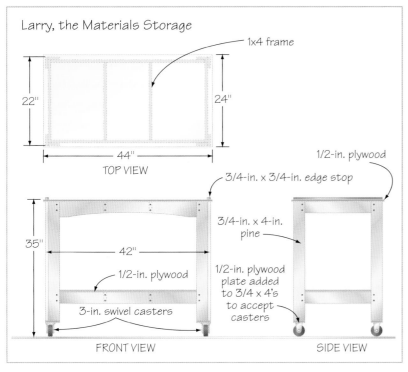

1x4 frame

22"

24"

44"

TOP VIEW

1/2-in. plywood

3/4-in. x 3/4-in. edge stop

3/4-in. x 4-in. pine

35"

42"

1/2-in. plywood

1/2-in. plywood plate added to 3/4 x 4's to accept casters

3-in. swivel casters

FRONT VIEW

SIDE VIEW

Curly, the Mobile Trash Bin

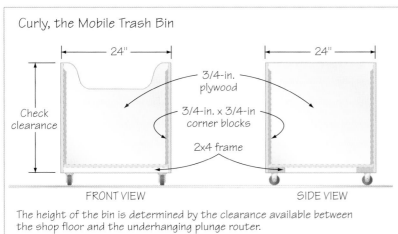

24"

24"

Check clearance

3/4-in. plywood

3/4-in. x 3/4-in corner blocks

2x4 frame

FRONT VIEW

SIDE VIEW

The height of the bin is determined by the clearance available between the shop floor and the underhanging plunge router.

5 | protect the shop's most valuable asset

You probably won't do this kind of work unless you really enjoy it. The hours are long, the tools are loud, the air isn't fresh and, sadly, there's no boss to hear grievances — but you love every minute of it. Perhaps too much: I rarely feel there are enough hours in the workday to accomplish what I'd like to do. There's nothing wrong with this energetic approach as long as your ambitions don't surpass your physical ability. At times the body is simply too tired, too mesmerized by the drone of the tools or too lacking in breathable air to work safely any longer. The situation can be exacerbated by illness, emotional distress and the ingestion of anything that overstimulates or depresses the nervous system.

Cabinetmaker's tools can be dangerous. For safety's sake, they must be operated by an aware mind and a healthy body. If you are not up to par, you must stop working. The stakes are simply too great.

Protective Clothing and Devices

Even on the best days, we need to protect ourselves from our machines and their by-products. The first thing I do when I enter the shop is don a work apron that covers most of my torso and keeps splinters and sawdust off my clothes. Look for an apron made of durable material with plenty of pockets and a strap design that takes the weight of the stash of tools and fasteners off your shoulders and puts it more comfortably around your waist.

Your feet also deserve consideration. While sneakers are comfortable, they offer insufficient protection from falling objects. I recommend lightweight, steel-toed work shoes with a padded arch-support insert.

Have you noticed how loud your tools are as they scream their way through the wood? You shouldn't (not because you're already deaf) because you should be wearing some form of ear protection. I use foam earplugs, which are effective and comfortable. (I find earmuffs to be uncomfortable over my glasses, and they make me feel claustrophobic.) Earplugs are inexpensive and can even be washed and reused. For me, the variety made from a highly supple foam with rounded ends feels the best. (Mine are made by Moldex-Metric Inc. See Appendix 1.)

When you work with fast, debris-spewing machinery, you must protect your eyes. Since I wear glasses anyway, I use a safety glass cut to my prescription and mounted in a sturdy frame. Side shields keep debris from sneaking in the sides. If you don't normally wear glasses, do so when you are in the shop. Goggles scratch quickly and are uncomfortable to wear for any length of time; you probably won't get into the habit of wearing them throughout the day.

You must also protect your lungs. The air in cabinet shops can be toxic to people who are allergic to certain wood species, glue substrates or finishing materials. The dust collection system and ceiling filter should eliminate a good deal of the airborn toxins, but when dust concentrations in the air become visible, you should wear a mask. The best mask I've ever encountered is the one made by Dust-be-gone (see Appendix 1). It features two flexible straps with Velcro closures, a washable shield membrane and an adjustable bridge to fit firmly and comfortably over the bridge of the nose. It's essentially a deluxe version of a useless single-strap dust mask. Another option is to wear a helmet equipped with a face mask and a battery-powered fan that blows filtered air over the face. I tend to use the helmet when I'm operating heavy machinery, as the face shield increases the protection.

If you deal with toxic fumes, a dust mask is ineffective; you need to wear a rubber-shield with a carbon-filter respirator. These respirators aren't very comfortable, but they do work. Change the filters regularly if you are exposed to high concentrations of fumes. Of course, the best protection comes from eliminating hazardous materials from the shop. In particular, avoid formaldehyde-laden particleboard and try to use water-based finishing products instead of solvent-based products (see chapter twelve).

To suppress potential fires, keep at least two fully charged type ABC fire extinguishers (good for all types of fires) in separate, readily accessible locations by the exit doors. Don't keep one near the stove, a likely source of a conflagration which may keep you from getting it when you need it most. Recharge when the indicator dial warns of a low charge.

First Aid

A well-stocked first-aid kit stored in an unobstructed area in the main portion of the shop is an absolute necessity. Buy a kit with a dustproof storage container. In addition to the usual assortment of bandages, sterile gauze pads and tape, include in the kit a tourniquet, scissors and a good pair of tweezers designed specifically for splinter removal (I also carry tweezers in my apron pocket). Since you might be alone when an accident happens, make it a point to learn basic first aid. Your local Red Cross chapter probably offers an inexpensive course. Let the instructor know what you do for a living; you may get some additional, shop-specific instructions. If you cannot get to a class, study a good book on first aid.

Because hand and eye injuries are common in woodworking shops, post phone numbers of doctors who specialize in these areas, along with the number of the closest emergency room, right next to the telephone.

Above all, be safety conscious and be careful. An old boatbuilder colleague (who still has all his fingers) once told me that every morning before going to work, he would look at his hands and promise "to bring 'em all home that night."

I keep a first-aid kit in a dustproof box near the sink. To be on the safe side, add an eye wash station there as well. Keep emergency phone numbers at the sink and by the phone.

It makes sense to keep all your senses safe: Goggles for vision, earmuffs for hearing, dust mask for smell (and respiration!) and gloves for touch. To keep taste buds happy, I always stock a Kit-Kat bar in my work apron.

the process

ONCE YOU'VE FOUND A SUITABLE SPACE IN A promising location and tuned up the tools and fixtures, it's time to pass out the cigars: A shop has been born. Before you slap the first switch and breath some life into this baby, give some thought to developing a highly productive work style — the next step in creating a successful woodworking livelihood.

To make the shop really work for you, and to enjoy the benefits of an efficient and sensibly paced production process, the sequence of tasks involved in building a set of cabinets must be carefully organized. You must scrupulously plan how materials will flow through the shop during the project. Products of one operation must not block access to the machinery and space requirements of the next operation. Components, related or not, must be grouped so that a particular tool setup need be created only once. Operations must be organized so that all materials reach the same production phase at the same time.

The following chapters present the production process I currently use in my shop. After an introduction to the elements of successful cabinet design and the "block production" method, each subsequent chapter represents a phase of the process. These phases, or production blocks, are graphically represented by flowcharts, which illustrate the relationship of steps within a block. The production process in its entirety is consolidated in the master flowchart that appears in Appendix 3.

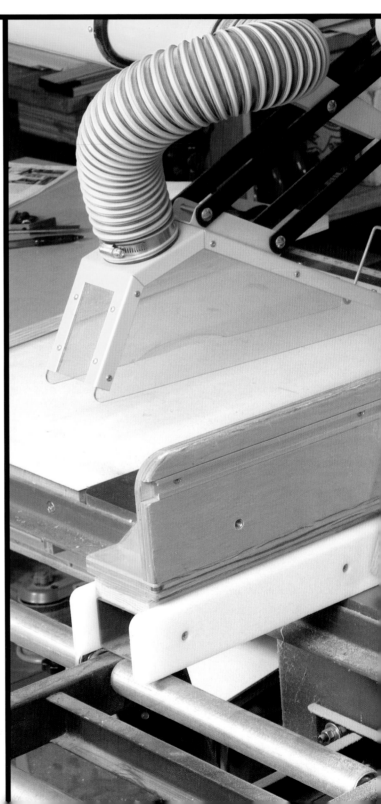

I carefully sequence the various stages of the production process to make the most efficient use of time, machinery and floor space. The payoff is greater productivity and profit — not to mention longer lunch breaks!

6 | cabinet design and block production

If you are not yet familiar with European-style cabinets, I suggest you find a showroom that has them on display and take a good look. The first thing you might notice is that the spacing between doors, drawer faces and fixed panels is extremely close, usually less than $\frac{1}{8}$". When you open the doors and drawers, you'll see the hardware that makes these close tolerances possible. Hinges are adjustable in three directions, drawer slides adjust up and down and even the fasteners that attach the drawer faces to their boxes allow adjustment. A screwdriver is all that is necessary to fine-tune the relationship of all the face components to each other.

Looking further, you'll find that the drawer slides and door-hinge mounting plates, as well as shelf-support clips and certain connection fittings (used to hold panels in place or the cabinets together), all fit into identical holes (measuring 5mm). The holes are spaced precisely 32mm apart in two vertical lines on the inner sides of each cabinet. These holes enable the cabinet sides to receive a variety of fittings, allowing any one component to hold many possible configurations of doors, drawers and adjustable shelves. Because the Europeans standardized their hardware systems (a result of restless German technology applied to the need for massive reconstruction of housing following World War II), they were also able to standardize cabinet components. The implica-tions of such standardization for the mass-production of cabinets are obvious.

While the technologists were adding these new hardware systems, the cabinetmakers were busy eliminating many traditional design features. Face frames and certain moldings were deemed unnecessary, as were integral kickboards and support frames (kickboards could be replaced with a facing board attached to adjustable leg hardware with clips). The final product was highly functional, straightforward and incredibly efficient to build.

It was also a pretty stark piece of work (some would even say sterile). The monolithic face presented by a run of European-style cabi-nets, broken only by fine lines between the unadorned, flat drawer faces and door fronts, offers little to please or interest the eye.

While the typical Euro-style cabinet can work well in a contemporary setting (and certainly in institutional applications), it can easily seem out of place in traditional-style houses.

In my adaptation of European construction methodologies, however, I have found no limit to the variety of styles that can be produced. As you can see in the photographs on page 43, the appearance of this kitchen is decidedly tra-ditional. Beaded panels, 19th-century-style cock beading and a variety of other molding elements abound, yet the cabinets' foundation is European contemporary.

I offer my clients a number of other styles of cabinetry as well, the majority of which are interpretations of traditional American designs, yet each is based on the same basic module using 32mm-system hardware. Each module is composed of two sides, a floor, a top frame (or sheet stock ceiling, if the cabinet is an upper unit) and a back. Before the module is assembled, the sides are drilled with the vertical rows of 5mm holes spaced 32mm apart. The first row is set back 37mm from the front edge of the case to accommodate the European cup hinge mounting plates and the front screws of the drawer slides. The second row is set back far enough to catch the rear mounting holes of the drawer slides. (For example, 22" slides require a 517mm setback.) Since I use European adjustable legs, I also drill holes for these in the cabinet floors before assembly. I don't have room in my shop to finish assembled carcasses (nor do I want to increase the overhead of my business by adding that room), so I prefinish the components of each module (in many cases, I buy the hardwood plywood already prefinished) and install all hardware before assembly.

This basic module serves as the foundation for any style of cabinet. A number of moldings can be used to augment and enhance the design and to tie the modules together visually. The cornice, light pelmet (which also serves to hide undercabinet lighting systems) and plinth offer strong horizontal lines that can bridge an entire run of cabinets, while pilasters, spacers and an applied midrail break up the spacing between face components.

In this type of cabinet, the exterior surfaces of the module sides are never seen: They are either hidden against a wall or another cabinet or covered with an applied panel. Using applied panels allows exposed ends of cabinet runs to mimic the style of the doors or to present a beautiful surface of solid wood.

Devoting some attention to these design elements when developing your own line of cabinetry will enhance the uniqueness and visual appeal of your product. I suggest beginning with large-scale (or even full-scale) drawings, and then building prototypes of the more promising designs. (See Appendix 2 for an excellent book on furniture design.) Do a good job when you build your prototypes: They may become product samples.

As you can tell, the way I developed my cabinet designs was profoundly affected by the cabinetmakers of postwar Europe. The challenge was coming up with a production process for custom woodworkers to build such cabinets within the parameters of humble spaces and modest tooling. Over the past several decades, through much thought, trial and error and help from tool manufacturers (who have recently put small-shop versions of high-tech industrial cabinetmaking tools within grasp), I have worked out my own solution to this challenge. I have even given it a name: the block production method.

These cabinets—a typical product of my shop—are a hybrid of traditional American styling and contemporary European construction methods and hardware systems.

A look inside one of the cabinets reveals the European cup hinges, adjustable 5mm shelf clips and corner-mounted drawer slides. All of these fittings are fixed into two vertical rows (one near the front of the cabinet, the other near the rear) of 5mm holes drilled in 32 mm increments.

This is a set of cabinets I built for a customer who wanted a truly traditional look. Notice the full-inset doors set into face frames and surrounded by cock beading (look this up on the Internet at your own risk!) Still, the hardware and construction methodology takes advantage of contemporary European systems.

The Block Production Method

For a small-shop operator to cope with the immensely varied, space-eating operations involved in producing a set of cabinets, it is necessary to use some form of consistent production methodology. The amount of time spent handling materials must be minimal, and operations should flow in a smooth, nonrepetitive stream. Operations must be organized so that products of previous operations do not hinder access to workstations. In meeting these goals, it's important to maintain control over the quality of the results.

My production method is based on a highly organized sequence of steps that details the processing of material from its entrance into the shop to its exit as a part of a finished cabinet unit. The premise of this methodology is that all the tasks involved in the manufacture of a set of cabinets can be grouped into exclusive process "blocks." It ruthlessly insists that all the materials intended to undergo a certain operation be grouped together, even if they are totally unrelated. Thus shelf edgings may find themselves in the company of drawer faces and door stiles in a crosscutting operation. Only one tool setup and subsequent space commitment is delegated to accomplish a major element of the production process. The blocks are carefully sequenced so that the material flows smoothly throughout the work space, and so that subsequent steps occur in the proper order.

The flowchart on page 45 shows the sequence and interrelationship of the production blocks. Of course, this representation is generalized, as each block shown on the chart actually contains its own, detailed flowchart. (See the illustrations that accompany the following chapters, and see the master flowchart in Appendix 3.)

In addition to the vast time savings that I have enjoyed from implementing the block production method, other benefits have also arisen. Because the processes are so clearly delineated within the context of any one project, it is possible to generate data that tells

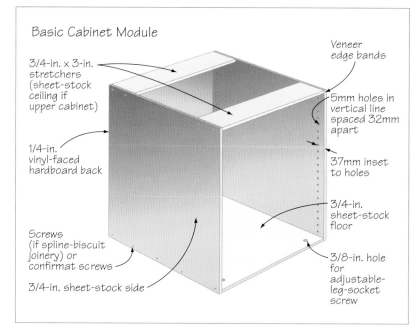

Basic Cabinet Module

3/4-in. x 3-in. stretchers (sheet-stock ceiling if upper cabinet)

1/4-in. vinyl-faced hardboard back

Screws (if spline-biscuit joinery) or confirmat screws

3/4-in. sheet-stock side

Veneer edge bands

5mm holes in vertical line spaced 32mm apart

37mm inset to holes

3/4-in. sheet-stock floor

3/8-in. hole for adjustable-leg-socket screw

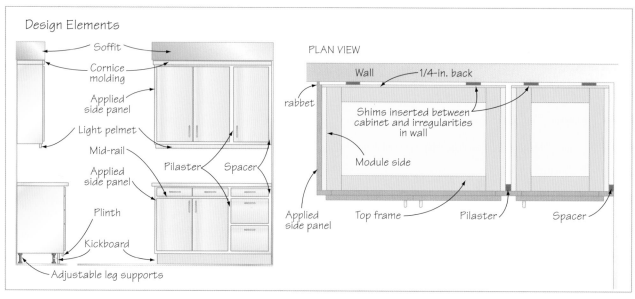

Design Elements

Soffit

Cornice molding

Applied side panel

Light pelmet

Mid-rail

Applied side panel

Pilaster

Spacer

Plinth

Kickboard

Adjustable leg supports

PLAN VIEW

Wall

1/4-in. back

rabbet

Shims inserted between cabinet and irregularities in wall

Module side

Applied side panel

Top frame

Pilaster

Spacer

the amount of labor required in any given process. (This is valuable information when estimating the costs of proposed projects; see page 109.)

Another benefit is that breathing space is automatically built into the pace of the work. Between blocks, you can recoup and clean up. To independent cabinetmakers working in humble spaces, this really makes a difference in the quality of the work life. Finally, once the block production method is firmly established in the shop, more than one project at a time can be done without confusion. A small job automatically nets a higher profit margin as it rides on the coattails of a larger project through the tool setups.

In the ensuing chapters of this section, the elements of the block production method are presented in the same sequence that occurs in the course of manufacturing a set of cabinets in a one-person shop. As you read, periodically refer to the master flowchart on page 126 to help you maintain a clear perspective of how each step relates to the whole process. I keep a large copy of the flowchart on the wall of my shop, lest I forget where to turn at the end of each production block.

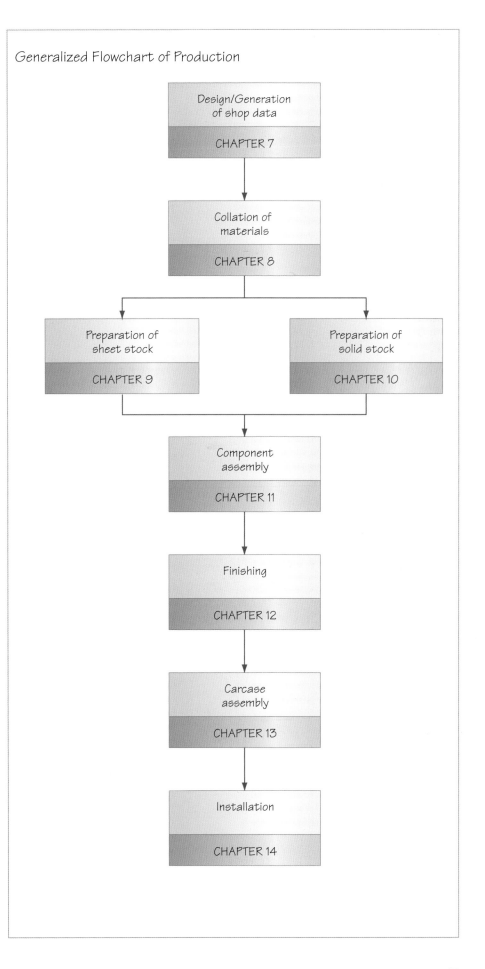

Generalized Flowchart of Production

Design/Generation of shop data — CHAPTER 7

Collation of materials — CHAPTER 8

Preparation of sheet stock — CHAPTER 9

Preparation of solid stock — CHAPTER 10

Component assembly — CHAPTER 11

Finishing — CHAPTER 12

Carcase assembly — CHAPTER 13

Installation — CHAPTER 14

7 | generate shop data

Any project invariably begins with a series of client consultations. The purpose of these meetings is to determine the exact specifications of the product you are to build. (For the benefit of all parties, this information should ultimately be in writing and signed by all the parties; see page 102.) During these consultations, you'll show the client photos of your products and samples of your standard door and drawer face styles. Note any unusual cabinet configurations, specialty hardware (such as lazy Susans and slide-out baskets) and the client's choice of decorative hardware on the rough elevation sketches. A box of sample woods is invaluable for helping clients choose the species they want for their cabinets.

If the client should ask you to design a new cabinet style, be aware that prototype development takes time and may require the purchase of additional tooling (such as router bits) and the construction of specialized jigs. You may choose to absorb these costs or pass them on to the client. Unless I know I will add a particular new style to my standard line, I charge the client for development time but absorb the cost of the tools, which will likely find other applications in my shop.

If the client hasn't already had a floor plan drawn up and the project involves more than one freestanding unit, the next design step is to lay out the project in plan view. If you have a talent for drawing, create a perspective view of the layout. If you can manipulate computer software, try one of a few kitchen design programs that create such views in about the same amount of time. Once you and the client agree on the layout, transfer any notations on cabinet configuration or specialty hardware from the rough elevation sketches onto a copy of the plans. Be sure that your contract with the client specifies the dimensions of each cabinet, any specialty hardware and the choice of style, wood species and finish.

Shop Drawings

Once you receive the go-ahead (and a deposit!), develop a scaled plan view of the project on vellum paper so blueprints can be made. This plan view, which looks directly down on the cabinets, details the relationship of the units and allows you to delineate the modules within each cabinet run. Again, if you like to work on computers, you can do this with a simple CAD program. More sophisticated rendering software — as seen in the screen shots on the next page — can give you a highly realistic representation of what the cabinets will look like when they are installed. This is a real boon for people who have difficulty picturing things from drawings, and it may save you much grief down the road!

Even if your client gives you a set of floor plans, you yourself should measure the space the cabinets must fit into. If the wallboard, final flooring or ceilings has not been installed, find out how that will affect your measurements. Also note anything else that might influence the design or installation of the cabinetry. Mark on your floor plan the exact placement of doors and windows if they will abut the cabinets; indicate any electrical or plumbing fixtures and note steps in floors or jogs in walls in the path of the cabinets. In addition, draw in the appliances, adding their model numbers and all pertinent dimensions. (Using the model numbers, you can double-check with the manufacturer the dimensions of any appliances not already on hand.)

After defining the modules, assign each an identification symbol or code for easy cross-reference in other shop drawings. (I use the first letter of the client's last name followed by a number. Thus the 12 modules built for Mrs. Smith have designations of S1 to S12.) Hang a blueprint of the drawing somewhere in your shop for reference throughout production.

Another necessary shop drawing set is an elevation of each module to be built. I do this on an elevation card (a 5" × 8" index card) that provides space for the drawing and a list of components and their dimensions. I keep these cards handy in a card box on Moe, the mobile tool cart.

Sometimes it is helpful to prepare elevations and cross sections of unusual details, such as built-up moldings. Be sure you have a side view of your standard cabinet component, including the spacing dimensions of the 32mm-system holes. Hang copies of these plans near the plan view of the job in progress.

Design and Generation of Shop Data

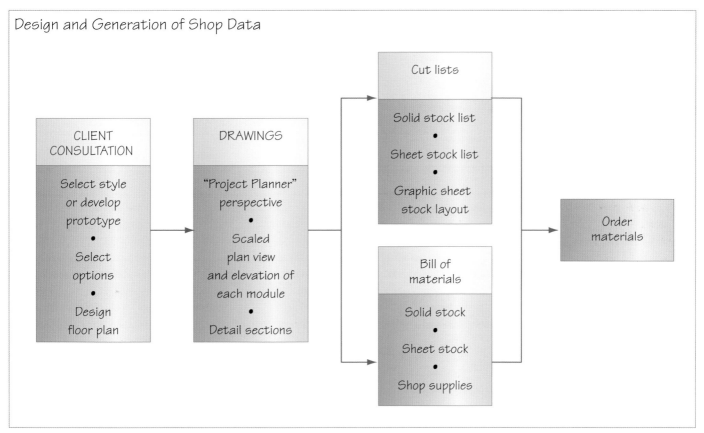

CLIENT CONSULTATION

Select style or develop prototype
•
Select options
•
Design floor plan

DRAWINGS

"Project Planner" perspective
•
Scaled plan view and elevation of each module
•
Detail sections

Cut lists

Solid stock list
•
Sheet stock list
•
Graphic sheet stock layout

Bill of materials

Solid stock
•
Sheet stock
•
Shop supplies

Order materials

An excellent way to help customers choose the wood species for their cabinets is to present them with a wide selection of real wood samples. You can make up your own sample box or purchase one (see Appendix 1).

Cutting Lists

Develop two cutting lists (one for solid stock and one for sheet stock) from the component information on each elevation card. Order the sheet stock components according to the type of sheet from which they'll be cut; thus, every panel to be cut from ³/₄" birch plywood gets listed under that category and arranged on a graphic representation of the 4' × 8' sheets, as shown in the figure on page 49. This step allows you to organize the panels to minimize waste, and it provides a fail-safe visual reference in the shop during actual panel sizing. Be sure to note the module designation and component function on each part.

Whenever possible, lay out the panels so that the initial cuts rip the sheets along their full length. This allows you to handle smaller sections of the sheets in subsequent sizing operations, ensuring a higher level of accuracy in the results.

Bill of Materials

To produce an order sheet for materials, compile the numbers from the cutting lists. First, total the board footage of solid stock needed; use the solid stock cutting list and a calculator with a memory function. By entering all the dimensions of the stock in feet (or fractions thereof), you can produce a sum representing the board footage.

For example, if a column of 1" × 4" stock adds up to 135 linear feet of material, enter this into the calculator's memory as 1 × .333 (the decimal equivalent of ⁴/₁₂ × 135). (The ⁴/₁₂, or .333, accounts for the fact that a 4"-wide board represents one-third of a board foot of material for each foot of its length.) Enter a column of 1" × 6" stock totalling 150 linear feet as 1 × .5 x 150. (If the components will come from stock thicker than 1", this must be accounted for. For example, if 4" moldings will be cut from 1½"-thick stock, enter this as 1.5 × .333 × the linear footage.) Simply recall the sum from the calculator's memory to get the total board footage of the material. When you order solid stock, however, always add at least 15 percent to the total board footage figure to compensate for defects and waste during processing.

To figure out the sheet stock order, count the types and quantities needed directly from the graphic representation. Order at least one extra sheet of each type for insurance in the event of a processing error.

Determine the hardware required by tallying the elevation cards, which list the doors, drawers, shelves and specialty items present in each module. Estimate incidental hardware such as connection fittings, cover caps and adjustable leg supports in relation to the size and complexity of the module. Remember that a project will also consume shop supplies not listed in the elevations or cutting lists. Estimate the amount of glue, fastenings, finish materials and applicators, sandpaper, steel wool and rags that you will need and replenish these supplies as necessary when ordering the rest of the material.

To avoid delays during production, order all the material needed for a project as soon as possible. If you have accepted a deposit while you are in the middle of another job, try to take a day off to make the elevation cards, cutting lists and bill of materials for the new project. Order the hardware immediately and arrange for your supplier to deliver the wood as soon as you clear the current project out of your shop.

Typical 5 x 8 Elevation Card

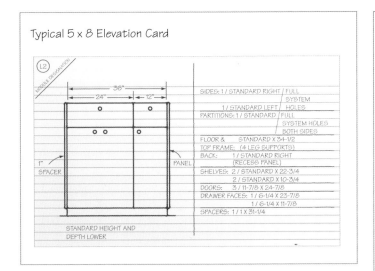

| SIDES: 1 / STANDARD RIGHT / FULL |
| 1 / STANDARD LEFT / SYSTEM HOLES |
| PARTITIONS: 1 / STANDARD FULL / SYSTEM HOLES BOTH SIDES |
| FLOOR & STANDARD X 34-1/2 |
| TOP FRAME: (4 LEG SUPPORTS) |
| BACK: 1 / STANDARD RIGHT (RECESS PANEL) |
| SHELVES: 2 / STANDARD X 22-3/4 |
| 2 / STANDARD X 10-3/4 |
| DOORS: 3 / 11-7/8 X 24-7/8 |
| DRAWER FACES: 1 / 6-1/4 X 23-7/8 |
| 1 / 6-1/4 X 11-7/8 |
| SPACERS: 1 / 1 X 31-1/4 |

1" SPACER
PANEL
STANDARD HEIGHT AND DEPTH LOWER

Typical Master Cut List for Solid Stock

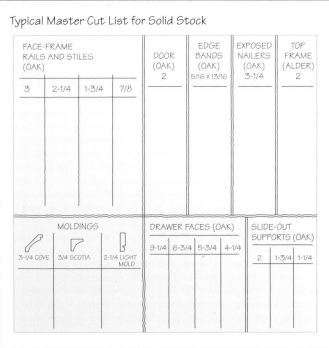

FACE-FRAME RAILS AND STILES (OAK)				DOOR (OAK) 2	EDGE BANDS (OAK) 5/16 X 13/16	EXPOSED NAILERS (OAK) 3-1/4	TOP FRAME (ALDER) 2
3	2-1/4	1-3/4	7/8				

MOLDINGS			DRAWER FACES (OAK)				SLIDE-OUT SUPPORTS (OAK)		
3-1/4 COVE	3/4 SCOTIA	2-1/4 LIGHT MOLD	9-1/4	6-3/4	5-3/4	4-1/4	2	1-3/4	1-1/4

Typical Graphic Sheet-Stock Layout for 3/4-in. Case Components

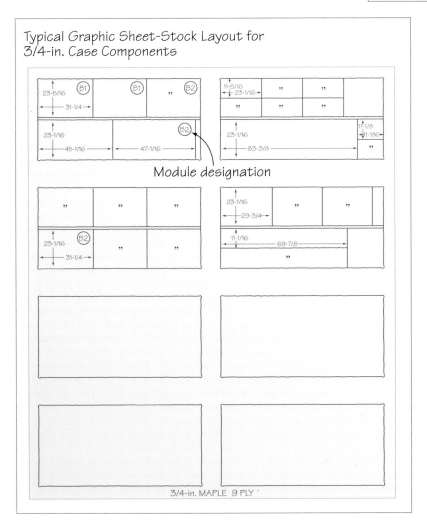

Module designation

3/4-in. MAPLE 9 PLY

collate and stack the materials

8

The diligent use of lumber racks and the multipurpose work platform helps prevent the small-shop gridlock that threatens at the beginning of each new project. Purging the racks and floor space of surplus stock and scrap also helps to prepare the shop for the arrival of materials. My rule is that solid stock measuring less than 2" x 2' and any plywood offcuts less than 2 feet square go either into the wood stove or into bundles to be donated to local hobbyists.

Organizing Your Materials

Clear the lower two levels of the lumber rack above the crosscut saw to receive the solid stock. When stacking the new lumber, separate it by thickness, placing the bulk of it (usually the 1" stock) on the first level. Reserve the level above it for stock of other thicknesses. To prepare for the sheet stock, place the multipurpose work platform on the 12" supports and orient it west to east in the shop. Except for the sheet material to be surfaced with laminate, all the incoming sheet stock will rest here. Lay the material to be laminated against the south wall of the shop to get that stock out of the way.

To keep production flowing smoothly, properly order the sheet stock that is stacked on the platform. The general rule in collating is that the material to be used last in the processing sequence should be at the top of the stack. Because the $\frac{3}{4}$"-thick sheets for the carcass components, including shelves and slide-outs, should go first in the next operation (predrilling system holes and other milling tasks), stack them on the bottom so they'll be sized last. After these sheets, the others follow this order: the $\frac{1}{2}$"-thick drawer side stock, $\frac{1}{4}$"-thick birch for drawer bottoms, $\frac{1}{4}$"-thick stock for recessed panels and $\frac{1}{4}$"-thick vinyl-faced stock for case backs. (Usually drawer fronts are made of solid stock, but if they are plywood, size them with the $\frac{3}{4}$"-thick carcass-component stock.) Then laminate the full-size sheets (if called for in the design for kickboards, backsplashes, etc.) and place them at the top of the top to be sized first.

As soon as the hardware arrives, count the pieces against the bill of materials for the project. If there is a discrepancy, check the packing slip for any items on back order or any error in fulfillment. Resolve deficiencies immediately to avoid delays when the production flow reaches the assembly blocks. Also check the quality of the hardware: Be sure you didn't get a knockoff version of the fittings. If you did and that's acceptable, be sure the price is right.

Except for large specialty items, store the hardware in the drawers of the sharpening station cabinets, which are located near the area used for case assembly. Commit one large drawer to drawer slides and divide its length into four bins. Use the two bins on the left to hold the left portions of your common slides (22" for standard kitchen lowers and 20" for vanity cabinets); use the two bins on the right to hold the right parts. Leave other lengths of drawer slides in their shipping cartons and store them in a separate drawer. Use another drawer to hold cup hinges and their mounting plates. Leave this drawer undivided and store the hardware, which can be quite varied in some projects, in its boxes. Put the adjustable legs and their sockets in the last drawer committed to hardware inventory, but keep the kickboard clips and cover caps separate. Store with them, in separate boxes, drawer-front adjusters, shelf supports, drawer bumpers, spacers and mounting sockets, bumper pads, and an assortment of installation fittings and cover caps.

Store the fastening hardware used in component and case assembly in the bins provided for this purpose on the side of Moe. Stockpile surplus fasteners in another drawer or put them in stackable plastic bins and store them in the upper cabinet above the sharpening bench. Now you're ready to jump into the production flow.

Collation of Materials

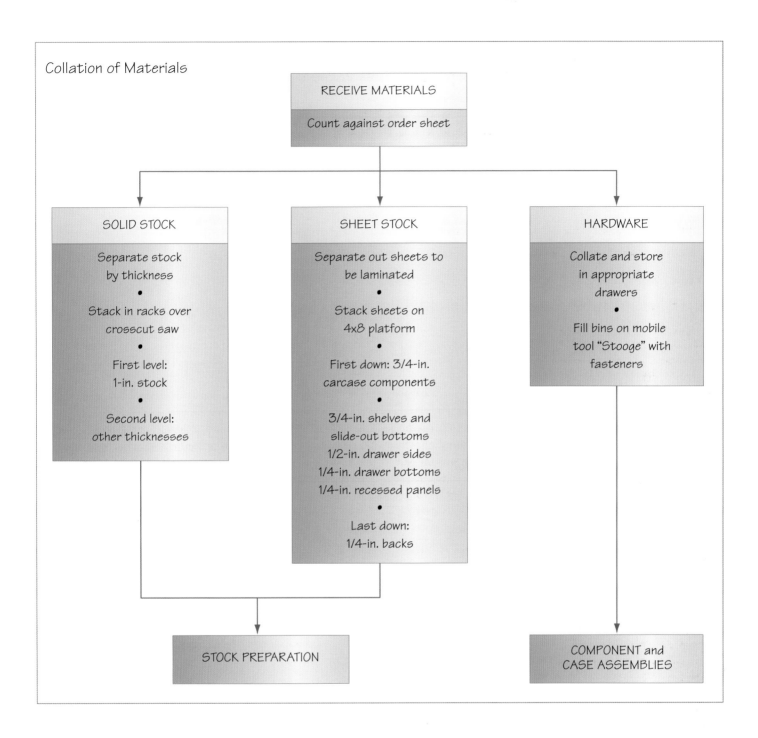

RECEIVE MATERIALS

Count against order sheet

SOLID STOCK

Separate stock
by thickness

•

Stack in racks over
crosscut saw

•

First level:
1-in. stock

•

Second level:
other thicknesses

SHEET STOCK

Separate out sheets to
be laminated

•

Stack sheets on
4x8 platform

•

First down: 3/4-in.
carcase components

•

3/4-in. shelves and
slide-out bottoms
1/2-in. drawer sides
1/4-in. drawer bottoms
1/4-in. recessed panels

•

Last down:
1/4-in. backs

HARDWARE

Collate and store
in appropriate
drawers

•

Fill bins on mobile
tool "Stooge" with
fasteners

STOCK PREPARATION

COMPONENT and
CASE ASSEMBLIES

9 | prepare the sheet stock

Preparing sheet stock is easily the most vigorous task you'll face in the construction of a set of cabinets. After sizing and stacking the twenty to thirty 4' x 8' sheets involved for an average-size kitchen and then doing the various milling operations (such as drilling rows of system holes, drilling shank holes for adjustable legs and slotting for spline biscuit joints), you'll have earned an afternoon off. Take one and enjoy it, for a third or more of the project has been completed.

Laminating Sheet Stock

If the project calls for components made of plastic-laminated sheet stock, you will likely have to laminate the sheets yourself or hire a subcontractor to do it for you; prelaminated sheet stock is limited in availability and color. (I usually use plastic laminate only for kickboards, but occasionally a client will ask for plastic-laminated doors and drawer fronts. If you choose to do it yourself, avail yourself of the method detailed in my book *Building Traditional Kitchen Cabinets*; this method enlists the force of gravity to help align the large sheets of laminate with the substrate. Another suggestion: The 3M company makes a water-based contact cement that really works (many water-based cements are relatively weak). It's nonflammable, nontoxic, not cheap — but well worth the money — commonly available from suppliers to the boat-building trade. You can also order it from any supplier that carries 3M products.

To achieve full bonding strength, you must mate the surfaces with a great deal of force. The force need be only momentary and can be achieved by applying firm pressure with a rubber roller (somewhat fun) or rapping a block and mallet over the entire surface (very boring). This is easiest to do with the sheet lying flat, of course, and an ideal location is the multipurpose platform, which is where the material must ultimately be located anyway. Thus, after each sheet is laminated (and remember you need to laminate both sides to maintain the dimensional stability of the stock), bring it to the platform for rapping or rolling. I use a simple, shop-built handling tool to make the job of maneuvering sheet stock a cinch (see the drawing on page 54). Save your back and invest less than an hour to build yourself one.

The Sizing Process

With all the sheet stock on the platform, you can begin running the material through the table saw. Well, you're almost ready. First, be sure the carbide-tipped plywood blade is mounted on the saw, and run a test piece to ensure the blade is sharp and not splintering out the underside of the cut, especially on the plastic laminate. Double-check the alignment of the rip fence to the plane of the blade, and adjust the shop helpers (see the photo on page 54) so that they hold the stock tightly against the fence without undue drag. (Note that you will have to readjust the helpers for different thicknesses of stock.) Referring to your sheet stock layout sketch, draw layout lines with a piece of chalk on the sheet on top of the pile. (You can eliminate this last step once you get into the swing of things and can recall the cutting pattern from a glance at the layout drawing.)

Begin by ripping the sheet lengthwise to the largest width specified by the layout, adding about $1/8$". Now turn the cut panel around, set the fence to the exact dimension and rip the sheet again running the first-cut edge against the rip fence. This strategy generally ensures the edges run true and parallel with one another.

Now crosscut the 8'-long pieces to length. If the panel is less than 18" wide, for safety and accuracy use a sliding table to carry the panel through the saw blade. This fixture (whether built or bought) will help crosscut the stock into components with ends at a true 90° to the ripped edge. Stock wider than 18" can be safely crosscut by running a trued factory edge against the rip fence. First test the factory edge for a true 90° with the jig shown on page 55. If necessary, proceed to true the edge using this same jig and a straight-cut router bit fitted with a top bearing. Slide the jig back on the panel to expose approximately $1/16$" to $1/8$" of the factory edge, and run the router along the arm of the jig. Once squared, the panels can be directly indexed to the rip fence and cut to exact length.

Continue to rip and crosscut all the sheet stock on the feed platform, stacking the sized panels on Larry to be carried to the east wall of the shop. Be sure to write the module designation and function (such as floor, side, etc.) in ink on the edge of each piece. (If the stock is less than $1/2$" thick, chalk this information on the surface near an edge.) Stack the panels so that these marks are visible.

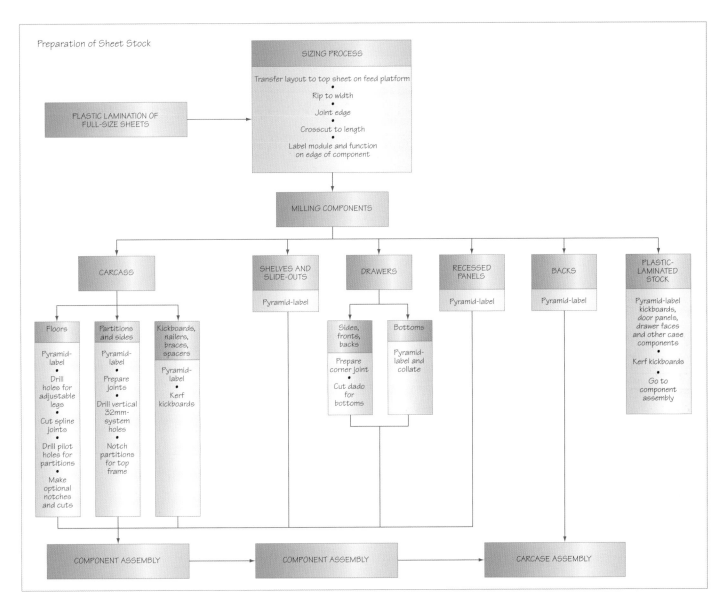

Preparation of Sheet Stock

SIZING PROCESS

Transfer layout to top sheet on feed platform
•
Rip to width
•
Joint edge
•
Crosscut to length
•
Label module and function
on edge of component

PLASTIC LAMINATION OF FULL-SIZE SHEETS

MILLING COMPONENTS

CARCASS

SHELVES AND SLIDE-OUTS

Pyramid-label

DRAWERS

RECESSED PANELS

Pyramid-label

BACKS

Pyramid-label

PLASTIC-LAMINATED STOCK

Pyramid-label kickboards, door panels, drawer faces and other case components
•
Kerf kickboards
•
Go to component assembly

Floors

Pyramid-label
•
Drill holes for adjustable legs
•
Cut spline joints
•
Drill pilot holes for partitions
•
Make optional notches and cuts

Partitions and sides

Pyramid-label
•
Prepare joints
•
Drill vertical 32mm-system holes
•
Notch partitions for top frame

Kickboards, nailers, braces, spacers

Pyramid-label
•
Kerf kickboards

Sides, fronts, backs

Prepare corner joint
•
Cut dado for bottoms

Bottoms

Pyramid-label and collate

COMPONENT ASSEMBLY

COMPONENT ASSEMBLY

CARCASE ASSEMBLY

As soon as you can afford to, add a sliding table to your table saw to allow you to make precise crosscuts in panel stock. Until then, you can make a crosscut box to carry the stock past the blade (see *Jim Tolpin's Table Saw Magic* for details).

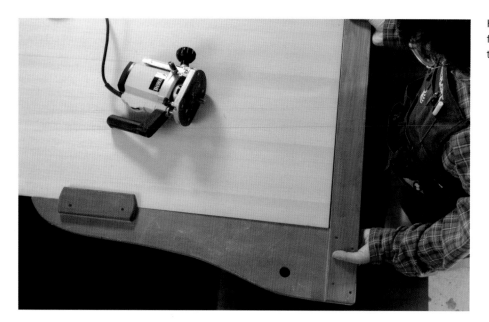

Hold the shop-built squaring jig against the factory-cut edge of a piece of sheet stock to check for a perfect right angle.

If the edge needs trimming, slide the jig back so that $\frac{1}{16}$" to $\frac{1}{8}$" of material is exposed past the jig arm at the narrowest point, then clamp it to the sheet. Using the arm as a guide, trim with a fluted router bit that has a top bearing mounted on the shank above the flutes.

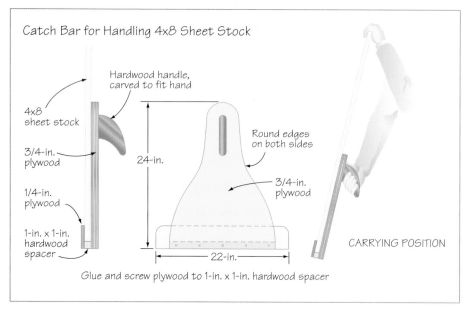

Catch Bar for Handling 4x8 Sheet Stock

Hardwood handle, carved to fit hand

4x8 sheet stock

3/4-in. plywood

1/4-in. plywood

1-in. x 1-in. hardwood spacer

24-in.

Round edges on both sides

3/4-in. plywood

22-in.

CARRYING POSITION

Glue and screw plywood to 1-in. x 1-in. hardwood spacer

Milling Carcass Components

Locate the sized carcass components, organize them by the functions they will serve (such as floors and sides) and stack them on 2×4s placed across two sawhorses. Rotate the multipurpose platform 90° (perpendicular to the table saw) and raise it up onto the 32" lifts to create a work surface for the following operations.

Begin with the floor components. As you bring each one up to the platform, orient it the way it will appear in the assembled case, mark its back edge with a portion of a pyramid and write the module designation beside it. This symbol will orient and identify the panel during the rest of its journey through the production process. If you see a pyramid, or a portion of one, on the edge of a component, you automatically know that it's the back edge; the portion of the pyramid shown reflects the type and orientation of the component. As shown in the drawing at right, below, the top half of a pyramid indicates a top, while the lower half indicates a bottom. Draw right or left portions of pyramids on sides, and draw full pyramids on vertical partitions.

Continuing with the floor components, locate and drill the holes that will receive the bolts for the adjustable legs; use the jigs shown on page 56. Use the same jigs to locate the legs along the back of the floor components.

The next step to perform on the floor components depends on the type of joint you will use to assemble the carcasses. If the units are to be of knockdown construction, you need do nothing further, as you will drill the pilot holes for the confirmat knockdown fasteners during case assembly. Stack the floor panels on Larry to be brought to the south wall of the shop for temporary storage.

If, however, you choose to use spline biscuit joints, this is the time to lay out and cut the slots. Prepare a layout guide to indicate the location of the center of each spline and also to act as a stop for the biscuit joiner while slotting in the middle of a panel for a partition. Your 36" back-to-back bench

clamp (see Appendix 1) can serve nicely as this layout guide. To prepare the clamp for this application, apply some masking tape where you will draw lines across the bar and down each side to indicate the center line of each biscuit slot. Begin the slotting process with partitions: Clamp the bar across the floor panel at the edge of partition location, then run the slotting machine into the floor at each slot center line

mark (see the photo on page 58). Be consistent: Always run the guide along the left edge of a partition (as seen from the face of the cabinet). Make the slots in the end of the partition by securing the clamp across the partition panel along its bottom edge and then running the machine against the clamp and panel end at the indicated marks.

Once you have cut the slots for the partitions, run a pilot hole sized for the

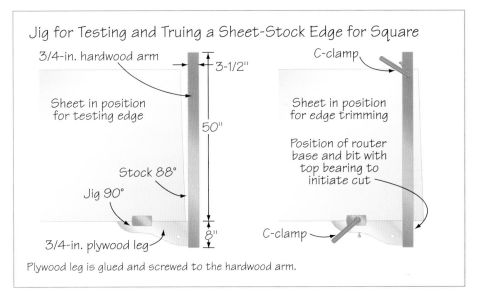

Jig for Testing and Truing a Sheet-Stock Edge for Square

3/4-in. hardwood arm

3-1/2"

C-clamp

Sheet in position for testing edge

50"

Sheet in position for edge trimming

Position of router base and bit with top bearing to initiate cut

Stock 88°

Jig 90°

3/4-in. plywood leg

8"

C-clamp

Plywood leg is glued and screwed to the hardwood arm.

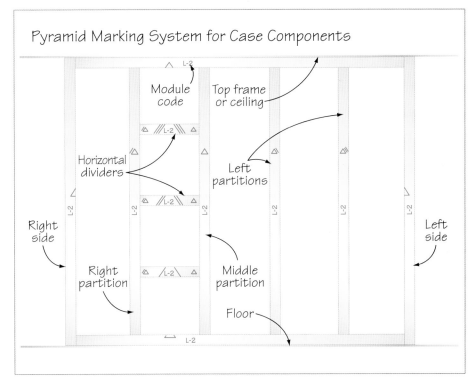

Pyramid Marking System for Case Components

L-2

Module code

Top frame or ceiling

L-2

Horizontal dividers

L-2

L-2

Left partitions

Right side

L-2

L-2

L-2

L-2

L-2

L-2

Left side

Right partition

L-2

Middle partition

Floor

L-2

screws to be used to draw the components together during assembly next to each slot. I have found that $1\frac{5}{8}$" drywall screws are ideal for this application. Except in laminated stock, they need no additional countersinking or pilot drilling to be installed. If any special cuts need to be made in the floors, such as a knee-clearance indentation in front of a sink area, make them now. When you have processed all the floor components and stacked them on Larry, roll them to the south wall of the shop to await edge-banding and finishing with the floor panels. Now load the side components onto the platform. If the case is to be joined with spline biscuit joints, continue the slotting process.

To slot the sides to receive floors, ceilings and top frames, clamp the layout guide to the side panel exactly $\frac{3}{4}$" (or the thickness of the stock to be joined) away from the edge. As when slotting for partitions, hold the spline biscuit machine vertically and plunge it down into the side stock. Since the face plate of the machine bears on only $\frac{3}{4}$" of material, place a strip of stock the same thickness as the side stock along the edge for support. If horizontal partitions will join the case sides,

A simple shop-built corner jig locates the holes in the cabinet floors for the adjustable legs. Stops on both sides of the jig allow it to be flipped over and used at the opposite corner. To minimize tear-out, use a sharp brad-pointed bit.

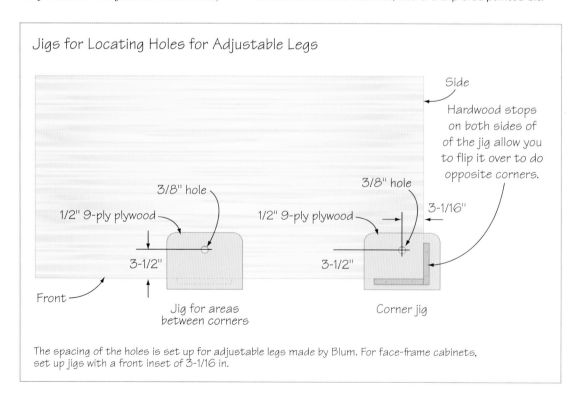

Jigs for Locating Holes for Adjustable Legs

Side

Hardwood stops on both sides of of the jig allow you to flip it over to do opposite corners.

3/8" hole

1/2" 9-ply plywood

3/8" hole

3-1/16"

1/2" 9-ply plywood

3-1/2"

3-1/2"

Front

Jig for areas between corners

Corner jig

The spacing of the holes is set up for adjustable legs made by Blum. For face-frame cabinets, set up jigs with a front inset of 3-1/16 in.

index the clamp guide consistently to the bottom of the partition.

The sides are now ready to receive their vertical 32mm-system holes. A commercially made router bit guide (see Appendix 1) allows you to quickly and precisely create a line of 5mm holes on 32mm centers. (For the price of a table saw, you can add to your drill press a line-boring head that bores five holes at once; for the price of a really good table saw, you can obtain a freestanding unit that bores up to 13 holes at a time. (See Appendix 1 for manufacturers.)

If the cabinets have face frames, you don't have to drill system holes for European-style hinge plates or drawer slides; these will attach directly to the sides of the face frame. In this case, you need only to drill the system holes in the areas that will have adjustable shelves. If, however, the cabinets do not use face frames to carry the door and drawer hardware, the sides and partitions must receive their full meas-

ure of system holes. To properly position these holes to receive hinge plates and drawer slides, they must be located a precise distance in from the vertical edge and up from the bottom. In all cases, the holes must be $1^{15}/_{32}$" (37mm) on center from the front edge of the cabinet. Remember to take into account any edge-banding that still has to be applied. The spacing from the rear edge of the panel is a function of the drawer slide length (hole spacing is standardized on slides throughout the industry) and the depth of the panel. For example, 22" slides provide for a rear screw setback of $18^{29}/_{32}$" (480mm) from the front screw. Simply lay out this spacing, then measure in from the back edge of the panel. The adjustable stops on the drill guide are set to the inset required; the base of the guide is always indexed to the bottom of the sides.

Jig partitions to receive the system holes in exactly the same way as the

When you are slotting for a partition intersecting the middle of a floor, the back-to-back clamp functions as a stop for the spline biscuit machine. The marks made on masking tape applied to the clamp locate the center line of each slot.

Here the machine cuts slots for the biscuits in a partition edge. The back-to-back clamp locates the center lines, while the work surface itself indexes the base of the machine. It's necessary to clamp the panel to the work surface.

When cutting slots near the end of a side panel to receive a floor, add a strip of material the same thickness as the side to help support the machine as it cuts in an upright position.

Drilling runs of 5mm holes in the side of a case is easily accomplished with a commercial jig. This one, by MEG Products (see Appendix 1), is unique in that it uses a router rather than a drill to create the holes. This means faster, cleaner, clog-free holes.

sides, except temporarily add a spacer of the same thickness as the floor stock to the base of the partition to catch the drill guide's bottom stop and maintain alignment. If notches are to be cut in the partitions, do this now with a jigsaw or band saw. (The band saw is faster and produces a more accurate cut.) Note that you can forgo notches if you size the partitions to fit between the floor and stretchers. Load the completed side and partition components on Larry and stack them with the floor components. Label remaining carcass components, such as nailers, spacers and braces, and take them to the south wall as well. (Note: Refer to the drawing of my shop on page 15 to orient yourself; your shop may not, of course, be oriented to the compass the same way mine is.) Give kickboards kerfs with a saw cut to receive the clips needed to mount them on the adjustable legs, then stack the kickboards with the nailers, spacers and braces.

If a number of similar notches need to be cut in partitions or side panels, set up a fence and stop on the band saw to guide and index the cut. Here I'm making the first cut, which I'll do on all the panels needing this notch. Reset the fence and stop before making the second cut.

Milling Other Sheet Stock Components

The stock that's up next in the stack against the east wall should be the ³/₄"-thick material for shelves and slide-outs. Label these and bring them to the south wall to await further processing (edge-banding for the shelves; assembly with solid side components for the slide-outs).

Next up in the stack are the ½"-thick drawer parts. Sort them into two piles — one for drawer sides, the other for fronts and backs — and place them on Larry. Wheel them to the shaping station and set up the router with a drawer-joint bit. (I use the one made by Freud; it's inexpensive yet makes a strong joint. See Appendix 1.) Shape a number of scrap pieces until you are satisfied with the joint. Rather than moving the fence to shape the joint on the drawer fronts and backs, use an auxiliary fence when routing the drawer sides, as shown on page 61. Secure a featherboard to the table surface to hold the components tightly against the fence.

Before leaving this workstation, remove the drawer-joint bit and chuck in its place a slotting bit to cut the dado slot for the drawer bottoms. Make a sample cut to make sure the inset from the edge and the depth of the dado are satisfactory (I use ⁵/₁₆" for both), then cut all the slots. Because the side of the component to receive the dado is always the side that has received the drawer joint, prepare the stock for an efficient feed process by orienting all the faces in the same direction. When the dado slotting is complete, wheel the components to the south wall of the shop and stack them away from the carcass components and shelves.

The last panels left in the east stack (unless plastic-laminated components are involved in the project) are the ¼"-thick drawer bottoms, recessed panels (if applicable) and carcass backs. Sand the drawer bottoms to 180 grit (unless, of course, you chose to use vinyl board) before labeling them and moving them to the stack of drawer components on the south wall. Sand the recessed panels with 220-grit sandpaper before stacking them in the area just to the left of the drill press. The case backs, assuming you are using a vinyl-faced material, need only be labeled. Then stack them with the rest of the carcass components.

Milling Laminated Panels

Depending on the job, face components, carcasses and kickboards will sometimes be made from plastic-laminated material. The sized components that will become doors need to be

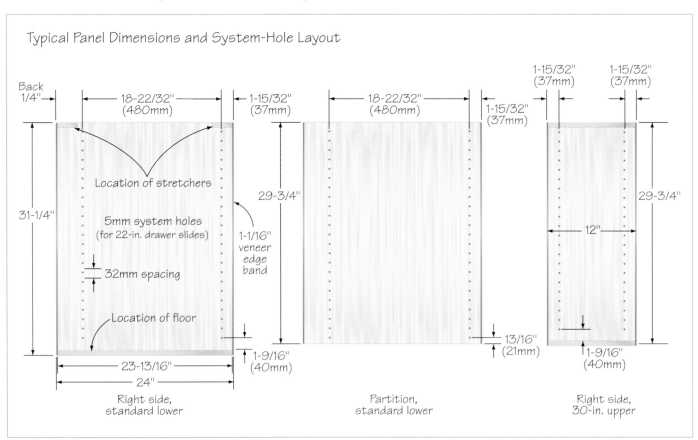

Typical Panel Dimensions and System-Hole Layout

Back 1/4"

18-22/32" (480mm)

1-15/32" (37mm)

Location of stretchers

5mm system holes (for 22-in. drawer slides)

32mm spacing

Location of floor

31-1/4"

1-1/16" veneer edge band

23-13/16"

24"

1-9/16" (40mm)

Right side, standard lower

18-22/32" (480mm)

1-15/32" (37mm)

29-3/4"

13/16" (21mm)

Partition, standard lower

1-15/32" (37mm)

1-15/32" (37mm)

1-15/32" (37mm)

29-3/4"

12"

1-9/16" (40mm)

Right side, 30-in. upper

edge-banded and drilled to receive cup hinges. Because this occurs in later production blocks, separate these pieces from the other sized panels and store them in a separate stack against the east wall. Also find the drawer fronts, which require edge-banding as well, and bring them to the south wall of the shop to await that process.

Run any strips of laminated stock earmarked for kickboards through the table saw to receive a ⅛" kerf along the length of the back. This kerf holds the press-in clips that attach the kickboard to the adjustable legs. Store the completed kickboards along the south wall of the

shop; you'll cut them to length and install them during the carcass-assembly production block (or during installation on projects that require the kickboards to span more than one module).

Pull any laminated panels destined to become carcass components from the stack and bring them up to the 2×4s set up by the multipurpose work platform. Refer to the elevation cards to determine which module and function each panel serves. Mark pyramid-labels on the components, and write the module codes on their edges. Perform the appropriate operations, and stack the panels along the south wall.

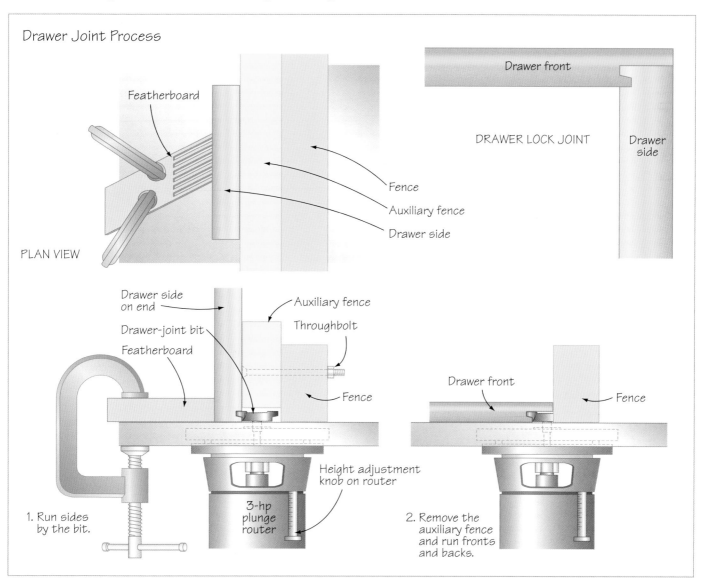

Drawer Joint Process

Featherboard

PLAN VIEW

Drawer front

DRAWER LOCK JOINT

Drawer side

Fence
Auxiliary fence
Drawer side

Drawer side on end
Auxiliary fence
Throughbolt
Drawer-joint bit
Featherboard
Fence

Drawer front
Fence

Height adjustment knob on router

3-hp plunge router

1. Run sides by the bit.

2. Remove the auxiliary fence and run fronts and backs.

10 | prepare the solid stock

There was a time in my shop when solid-stock preparation was more than a production block; it was, in fact, practically the entire process. In addition to doors, drawer faces and face frames, I built case sides, shelving, drawer boxes and even countertops from solid wood. I made only cabinet floors and backs from sheet stock.

The tedious processes of working with solid stock filled my shop with fragrance but did little to fill my pockets with cash. I was really building furniture and calling it cabinetwork. As you just saw in the previous chapter, I now make up much of the casework from sheet stock. Solid stock, however, still remains my material of choice for doors and drawer faces, end panels, face frames and other components such as moldings, exposed nailers and edge-banding for shelving. Solid stock is also best for accessories including door-mounted bins, appliance garages and exposed shelving, which further contribute to the warmth and quality of the cabinetry.

Surface Planing

When you order solid stock, ask your suppliers to plane it to $1/8$" over the finished dimension you need and not to joint the edges (this stock is referred to in the trade as S2S, that is, "surfaced two sides"). Doing the final preparation yourself is the only way to ensure that you will have smooth, uniform material to work with.

Prepare for planing by moving the multipurpose platform to the southern half of the shop and setting it on the 32" lifts. Set the surface in the middle of the platform, running lengthwise. Hook up the vacuum hose to the dust chute. Now round up Larry and load up the stock stored on the first rack above the radial-arm saw (this is typically the 1" stock planed by your supplier to $7/8$"). Wheel the stock to the platform and position it down to the right of the planer as you face the infeed. If you need more room for the stock than is provided by the platform, insert 8'-long 2×4s crosswise between the platform and the planer support grid.

For the smoothest possible surface, set the planer to cut off only $1/32$" of wood at each pass. Verify that the blades are sharp; if they're not, take 20 minutes to hone the blades on your waterstones.

When everything is ready, feed the stock through and stack it to the left of the planer. Lower the cutterhead to remove another $1/32$" and feed the material through once again, flipping the boards to expose the opposite surface to the blades. Repeat the process until you have the desired dimension. I surface 1" stock down to $13/16$". This allows more definition to be shaped into the molded edges of doors and drawer faces than would be possible with $3/4$" stock. Another advantage is that edge-banding can be ripped from the stock in one operation.

Layout

I always anticipate the layout stage of the production process with some trepidation. Faced with a pile of boards of varying widths and lengths, the task is to discover the most productive way to lay out all the components that must come from this wood. I try to tackle this project with a fresh mind and a positive attitude.

Try to eliminate as much material as you can as quickly as possible (before your brain cells overheat). Begin by sorting through the pile, culling out the widest pieces of stock. Spread these out across a pair of 32" lifts, then retrieve the solid stock cut list. Since the list is broken down by widths, it is simple to assign the widest components to the widest stock. Chalk the layout lines directly on the stock, allowing at least 1" of waste at the board ends. Take care to avoid defects in the wood. Many of the wider components are drawer faces; laying out adjoining drawers on the same board yields a pleasing flow of grain patterns from one cabinet to the next. A bank of drawers can be laid out and grain matched by edge laminating enough stock to form a panel 1" longer and 1" wider than the combined height of the faces. This panel will be ripped to the required individual widths after surfacing.

Other components to come out of the wide stock are the boards to make up other edge-laminated panels, if they are called for in the project. You will find that a significant amount of board footage rapidly becomes committed. The task begins to take on a more manageable proportion.

As you continue through the cutting list, try to select door rail and stile stock from the straightest wood left in the pile. Also, if you must make any paired doors, try to lay out adjoining stiles on the same length of stock, then rip it into two pieces. This allows the grain to match perfectly from door to door, and any movement in the wood will occur in a similar way in each stile.

Whenever possible, try to group components of similar length on the stock so you can roughly crosscut them to length in the same operation. This is especially helpful with stock that has a significant amount of curve to the edge; the board yields more width if it needs to be straightened only over portions of its run, as shown below. Note the straight reference lines, which indicate where to begin the first rip. Repeat these layout steps for each thickness of stock to be used in the job.

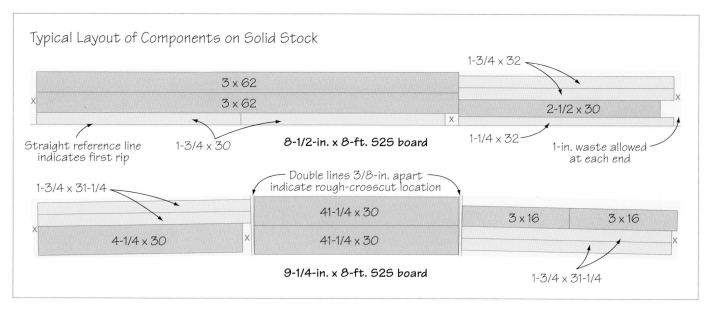

Typical Layout of Components on Solid Stock

Preparation of Solid Stock

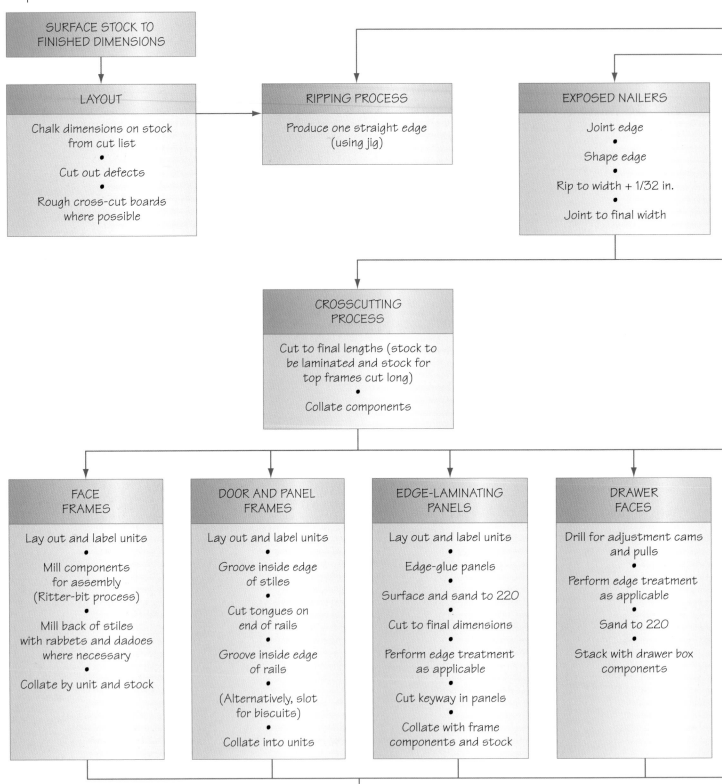

SURFACE STOCK TO FINISHED DIMENSIONS

LAYOUT

Chalk dimensions on stock from cut list
•
Cut out defects
•
Rough cross-cut boards where possible

RIPPING PROCESS

Produce one straight edge (using jig)

EXPOSED NAILERS

Joint edge
•
Shape edge
•
Rip to width + 1/32 in.
•
Joint to final width

CROSSCUTTING PROCESS

Cut to final lengths (stock to be laminated and stock for top frames cut long)
•
Collate components

FACE FRAMES

Lay out and label units
•
Mill components for assembly (Ritter-bit process)
•
Mill back of stiles with rabbets and dadoes where necessary
•
Collate by unit and stock

DOOR AND PANEL FRAMES

Lay out and label units
•
Groove inside edge of stiles
•
Cut tongues on end of rails
•
Groove inside edge of rails
•
(Alternatively, slot for biscuits)
•
Collate into units

EDGE-LAMINATING PANELS

Lay out and label units
•
Edge-glue panels
•
Surface and sand to 220
•
Cut to final dimensions
•
Perform edge treatment as applicable
•
Cut keyway in panels
•
Collate with frame components and stock

DRAWER FACES

Drill for adjustment cams and pulls
•
Perform edge treatment as applicable
•
Sand to 220
•
Stack with drawer box components

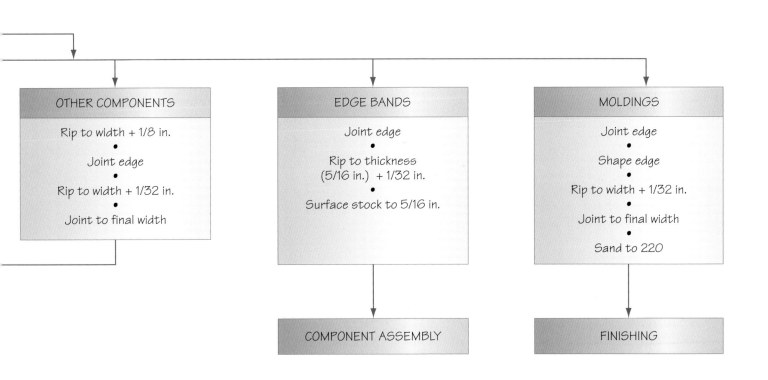

OTHER COMPONENTS

Rip to width + 1/8 in.
•
Joint edge
•
Rip to width + 1/32 in.
•
Joint to final width

EDGE BANDS

Joint edge
•
Rip to thickness
(5/16 in.) + 1/32 in.
•
Surface stock to 5/16 in.

MOLDINGS

Joint edge
•
Shape edge
•
Rip to width + 1/32 in.
•
Joint to final width
•
Sand to 220

COMPONENT ASSEMBLY

FINISHING

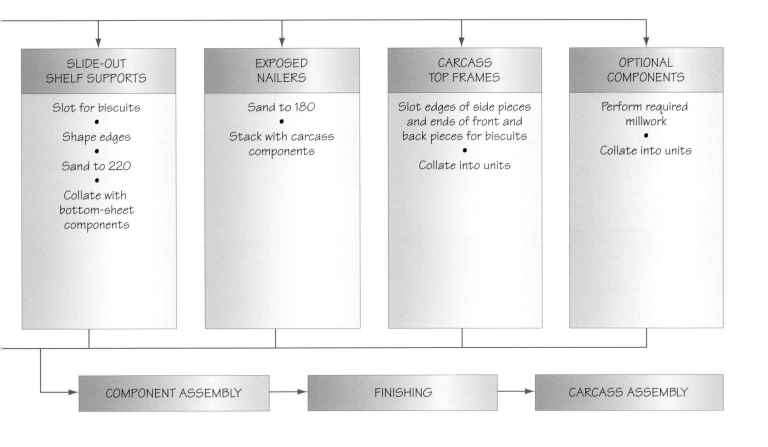

SLIDE-OUT SHELF SUPPORTS

Slot for biscuits
•
Shape edges
•
Sand to 220
•
Collate with bottom-sheet components

EXPOSED NAILERS

Sand to 180
•
Stack with carcass components

CARCASS TOP FRAMES

Slot edges of side pieces and ends of front and back pieces for biscuits
•
Collate into units

OPTIONAL COMPONENTS

Perform required millwork
•
Collate into units

COMPONENT ASSEMBLY → FINISHING → CARCASS ASSEMBLY

Ripping the First Straight Edge

In preparation for ripping, roughly crosscut the boards where possible. Rather than hauling them over to the radial-arm saw, I just crosscut the boards with a jigsaw as they sit on the lifts.

To avoid freehanding the stock through the table saw, rip the first straight edge on each board using the method shown below. Make sure the edges of the hardwood straightedge are perfectly straight and parallel. Rip the board by running the straightedge against the rip fence, with the blade set to cut just to the left of the reference line.

Ripping Edge-Banding and Moldings

Now sort through the lumber pile and pull out all the boards designated for edge-banding and moldings. Ripping this stock is a little different from processing the other components.

Begin with the edge-banding. Run the ripped edge of the first board over the jointer, removing just enough material to get rid of the saw marks. (It isn't critical that the board be jointed perfectly straight.) If the stock is thicker than the $\frac{3}{4}$"-thick sheet stock it will have to band, you only need to rip it once at $\frac{5}{16}$" plus $\frac{1}{32}$" to produce edge-banding. If it is not thick enough to provide an overhang for trimming, rip the stock twice: once at $1\frac{3}{16}$" then again in half to produce two $\frac{5}{16}$"-plus edge-bands. You may need to use a thin-kerf rip blade or a band saw to get two $\frac{5}{16}$"-plus pieces out of $\frac{3}{4}$" stock.

Use shop helpers or shop-made hold-downs to hold the stock down on the table tightly against the rip fence. Use a push stick as shown at right to move the edge-banding offcuts through the blade; keep the push stick parallel to the table to get under the arms of the shop helpers. As each band is cut off the board, joint the rough edge of the parent material and rip out another band. Continue until you've milled them all.

Let the jointer, table saw and dust collector run continuously throughout this operation. This saves wear and tear on the motors, which strain against inertia every time they start up. This also saves a little time from not fumbling for switches, and it fills your shop with the sweet sounds of progress.

The next step is to run the bands through the surface planer to true the stock to exactly $\frac{5}{16}$" in thickness. With that done, stack the completed edge-banding with the carcass components along the south wall and put away the planer.

Preparing moldings and exposed nailers (which you can see in the top rear corner of upper cabinets) is a similar process to that used for the edge-banding, except it is necessary to shape the edges of the stock between jointing and ripping. (Thus, yet another machine is added to the symphony of progress.) Smooth the rough edges of the parent stock on the jointer. Run the smoothed edge by the shaping cutter. Rip the molding or exposed nailer to its width plus $\frac{1}{32}$" and set aside. Repeat until all moldings and exposed nailers are complete. Run the pieces over the

---

Creating a Straight Line on Rough Solid Stock

Hardwood straightedge tacked to stock with drywall screws at each end (in 1-in. waste sector)

Rip fence

Blade

D

D

Reference line

The straightedge is located on the stock so that D = D. The right edge of the stock must not protrude beyond the right side of the straightedge.

To make precise, safe rip cuts in solid stock, I set up my shop-made fence fixture with featherboard hold-downs as well as a shop-made side hold-down that locks into the miter gauge slot. I use an aftermarket throat plate fitted with a splitter to ensure the kerf doesn't close back up on the blade. I use a push stick held flush to the table to push the stock the rest of the way through the blade.

jointer to remove the extra $\frac{1}{32}$"; using push sticks with nonslip surfaces, not your hands, to move the stock past the cutterhead. Sand the moldings to 220 grit and set them out of harm's way on the lumber racks until it's time to finish them. Stack the exposed nailers on Larry in preparation for crosscutting.

Ripping the Other Components

Rip the balance of the stock for face frames, carcass frames, door and panel frames, drawer faces and edge-laminated panels to width in a similar fashion. Begin with wider stock and work your way down to the narrowest components. Use the hardwood straightedge shown in the drawing on page 66 to rip the initial straight edge on each board. Then rip to the required width plus $\frac{1}{8}$". (Don't bother jointing the edge between subsequent rips.)

Once you have processed all the stock, sort the material into piles based on width. Beginning with the widest stock, joint any bow out of the board (which is why you provided that $\frac{1}{8}$" of extra width). If the board is so bowed that jointing will decrease the width below the desired dimension, crosscut the stock at the layout marks with your jigsaw and then joint the remaining bow out of the edge. Proceed to rip the stock to final width plus $\frac{1}{32}$". Finish the operation by jointing this $\frac{1}{32}$" off the rough edge. Continue the process until you've dimensioned all the boards and stacked them onto Larry, then wheel the load over to the east wall of the shop between the radial-arm saw and the drill press. Leave the material on Larry for now.

The Crosscutting Process

Bring the multipurpose platform and lifts over to where you parked Larry. Sort the material by length, removing the boards that contain the longest components to be cut and stacking them to the left of the platform. Continue to sort until all the material has been transferred from the cart to the platform. The last pieces stacked to the right side of the platform should contain the shortest components. Roll the empty cart near the radial-arm saw to receive the components as they're cut.

Now set the sliding stop on the radial-arm saw fence to the greatest length required and begin crosscutting. Work your way through each stack toward the shortest lengths. Cut all the components to the exact dimensions specified by the layout. The exception is stock to be edge laminated into panels or banks of drawer faces and stock for top frames: Give these components an additional $\frac{1}{2}$". When the last part has been cut, roll Larry up to the platform again and sort the parts by function: face frames, door frames, fixed panel frames, carcass top frames, exposed nailers, drawer faces and panel stock.

Face-Frame Preparation

Remove everything but the face-frame parts from the platform and stack them in their respective piles against the shop's east wall. Now, using the elevation cards, sort the face-frame components into modules, orienting and labeling the pieces using the pyramid system (see page 55). Keep in mind that face frames often extend over more than one module. Position the piles to the north end of the platform; if you need more room, use Larry's top shelf.

When a project calls for face frames, I find that the simplest, fastest way to make the frame joints is with pocket screws. (See Appendix 1 for suppliers.) Make the joint by drilling the pocket holes with a specialized drill and fixture and then gluing and fastening the parts together with special screws. The juncture of the shank with the head on these screws is absolutely square, thus they will not split out the end grain. The resulting joints are extremely strong, require very little surfacing to become flush and, best of all, require no clamping while the glue dries.

Begin the drilling process by orienting the components of a face frame into the configuration that is shown on the elevation card for the module. To indicate where to drill, mark the back surface of each end that butts into another. Pile the marked pieces onto Larry and roll them over to the work platform. Set each component into the jig and drill the holes. Components $1\frac{1}{4}$" to $2\frac{1}{4}$" wide get two holes, while narrower stock gets only one. Wider stock can get a hole every $\frac{3}{4}$" to $\frac{7}{8}$".

Once you've drilled the face frames for each module, integrate the drilled pieces with the rest of the module's pieces, which you left on the platform. (If stiles that abut walls need a rabbet to make fitting easier; do it now.) Wrap a piece of tape around the pile to hold it together. Repeat this process for each face-frame unit.

Preparation of Door and Panel Frames

Bring all the boards for these pieces to the multipurpose platform and sort them into units as specified on the elevation cards. Lay out each unit in its final configuration; use the pyramid labels to orient and identify each component.

The next steps depend on the style of door and panel called for in the project. I currently offer two types of frame and panel door: The first uses a variety of sticking (grooving) and coping router bits to create molded tongue-and-groove joints (the dado for the panel is cut at the same time). The second type uses the spline biscuit machine to create the frame joints and the applied moldings to contain the panel. The latter method allows me to create unique doors, as I can develop my own bolection moldings to trim the inner edge of the frames.

To produce either type of door, the first step is to sort the frame components into two stacks: rails (the horizontal pieces) and stiles (the vertical pieces). If the tongue-and-groove joint is to be used, bring the stiles to the shaping area and stack them on the table saw's outfeed table. Install the sticking (grooving) bit in the router and run test samples until you are satisfied with the placement and depth of the groove. (This is another good time to use shop helpers.) If you use the table saw's rip fence as the shaper fence, simply slide the hold-downs out of their mounting brackets and reinsert them from the opposite direction. Adjust them for the thickness of stock you are running.

When the setup is ready, run all the inside edges of the stiles by the cutter (to prevent tear-out, the rails will also get this cut but not until after the tongues have been cut). Bring the completed stack of stiles to the platform and gather up the rail stock. Stack this on the outfeed table, install and tune up the coping bit, and run the ends of each rail by it. Use a square piece of solid stock with a push stick to back the rails through the cut, preventing tear-out and keeping the stock square to the fence.

When all the rails have been coped, reinsert the sticking bit. Tune it up again on scrap, then process the inside edge of the rails. Bring the completed stock to the platform and sort the rails and stiles into their respective units. Tape them together and stack them on the east wall to the left of the drill press.

Process the second type of door using spline biscuit joints on the platform. I use a shop-made fixture, as shown in the drawing on page 69, to perform this operation. Doubling the splines at each joint increases the strength of the connection, though this is not usually necessary in ¾"-thick doors. To do this, first run the machine into the wood with the base resting on the jig's work surface. For the second cut, rest the machine on a ³⁄₁₆" plywood spacer as shown at bottom right. The stationary machine simply requires that the table be reset to provide a second slot at a different level. Once all the stock has been slotted, sort and bundle it into units and stack it along the east wall.

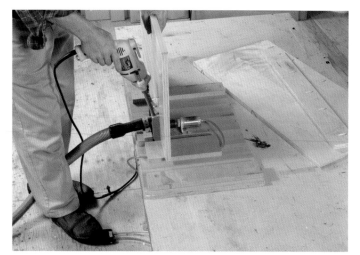

I use a commercial fixture to create pocket screw holes. This tool made by the Kreg Tool Company (see Appendix 1), employs a foot-pedal-actuated pneumatic clamp to hold the stock securely in place. A dust chute pulls the chips away from the cutting action.

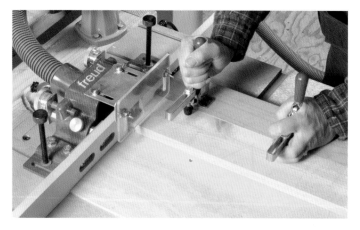

A shop-made carriage outfitted with toggle clamps is essential for making safe and accurate coping cuts on the table-mounted router.

I use a miniature power feeder to carry stock by the router for the sticking (grooving) cut.

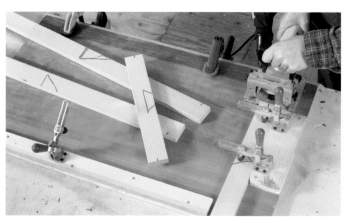

I use this shop-made fixture to hold stock for spline-biscuit slot cutting. Here I'm making a slot in the end of a work-piece.

Preparation of Panels

Now bring the stock that you will edge laminate into panels to the multipurpose platform for sorting and marking. Also be sure to bring the stock for building any panels from which a bank of drawer faces may be created. Align the boards with an eye to creating a pleasing match of grain across the panel's width. I have found that if the stock has been properly dried, (that is, if it has less than 6 percent to 8 percent moisture content) you can safely ignore the orientation of the stock in regard to the direction of the growth rings on the ends of the boards. When you are satisfied with the appearance of the panel, use chalk to mark a large pyramid on the surface that spans all the boards; write the module code in the center.

To create an efficient way to hold multiple 1" pipe clamps in position for the lamination process, rip out two clamp supports from a 2×6 board into which you've drilled a line of $1^{1}/_{4}$" holes every 8" along its center line. Put the two boards across a pair of 32" lifts. The half circles securely cradle the pipe clamps, keeping them parallel and level with one another.

Prepare to glue the stock by laying down all the pipe clamps that will fit onto the clamp supports. Distribute the panels along the pipe clamps. If certain lengths of panel fall short of the 8" spacing of the pipes, don't center the panel; instead keep a clamp under one extreme end and add a clamp to the top of the panel at the other end. To keep very wide panels from buckling, lay clamps over the top.

Roll glue onto the surfaces of the first panel to be joined with a self-spreading glue applicator (see Appendix 1). Don't overdo it; an overly thick coat will just squeeze out under pressure and waste glue. The perfect amount of glue beads uniformly along the joint under pressure yet does not drip significantly. Apply clamping pressure starting at one end and work toward the other, aligning the board's surfaces with a plastic or rubber mallet as you go along. Be careful not to over-tighten the clamps; that will cause all the glue to run out of the joint. If you suspect that certain panels will give you trouble because of opposing deflection in the adjoining boards, use spline biscuits to align the pieces.

Chalk the time on each panel as it is glued up, and continue to laminate until you run out of clamps. If your shop is warm and you have just the right number of clamps, you may experience one of those sweet moments in cabinetmaking when everything goes just right: The first panel will be ready to unclamp just as you have used the last pipe clamp.

Remove the excess glue from the panels right after taking off the clamps (usually within two hours of the initial clamping when an aliphatic resin glue is used and your shop is warmer than 65° F). If you dally and let the excess glue become brittle, it will invariably take small but deep chunks of wood with it when you scrape it off.

Once the glue has reached full

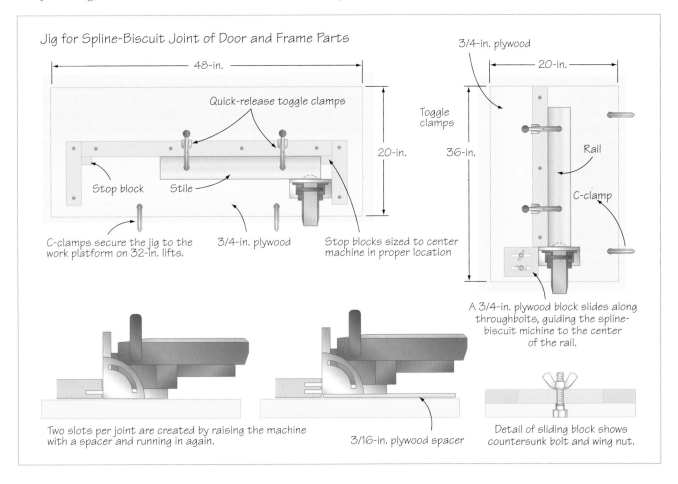

Jig for Spline-Biscuit Joint of Door and Frame Parts

48-in.

Quick-release toggle clamps

3/4-in. plywood

20-in.

20-in.

Stop block

Stile

Toggle clamps

36-in.

Rail

C-clamp

C-clamps secure the jig to the work platform on 32-in. lifts.

3/4-in. plywood

Stop blocks sized to center machine in proper location

A 3/4-in. plywood block slides along throughbolts, guiding the spline-biscuit michine to the center of the rail.

Two slots per joint are created by raising the machine with a spacer and running in again.

3/16-in. plywood spacer

Detail of sliding block shows countersunk bolt and wing nut.

strength (the next day is ideal), surface and smooth the panels. If you have a lot of them, consider taking them to a commercial shop that has a wide-belt thickness sander. It will cost you, but the labor you save should allow you to do more work (probably more enjoyable work) over the course of a year, and the results should leave the panels ready for final sanding. Before running the panels through the machine, remember to transfer the module code from the faces to the edges.

If you must surface the panels yourself, do so on a good worktable. Position a pair of 32" lifts in the open space in the southern half of the shop, set up the multipurpose platform and screw a piece of plywood approximately 32" wide and 48" long to it. Clamp a pair of back-to-back clamps across the plywood to hold the panels securely for surfacing. (See the photos on this page.)

Depending on your energy level, you can use planes and cabinet scrapers or a belt sander for this operation. Planing and scraping are highly taxing, even when the tools are extremely sharp and their beds have been waxed to reduce friction. However, I think that it actually goes more quickly than belt sanding. I'm quite sure the surfaces end up flatter, and I know that it's a lot quieter. Finally, the finish presented by a

I clamp the workpiece against the back fence of the fixture for slotting the edge.

I drill a 2x6 board with a row of $1\frac{1}{4}$" holes spaced 8" apart along its center line, then rip it in half to create two 2x3 pipe clamp supports. The resulting half-circles hold the clamps parallel to and level with each other and allow me to clamp long panels or a few shorter panels at the same time.

To secure a panel for surfacing with hand planes, fasten two back-to-back clamps to a piece of plywood, which is, in turn, screwed to the work platform. Begin surfacing with a No. 4 smooth plane that you have set coarse and shoot it at a diagonal across the panel.

The second step in planing a panel flat is to run a No. $4\frac{1}{2}$ plane with the grain and parallel to the edge of the boards. Set it to take a finer cut than that taken with the No. 4 plane.

planed surface versus that of a sanded surface is noticeably richer and deeper looking.

If you decide to plane, start with a No. 3 or No. 4 smooth plane set to take a coarse shaving, then follow with a No. 4½ smooth plane (a wider version of the No. 4) set to take a fine shaving. Use an 800-grit waterstone to knock the corners off the plane blades to avoid grooving the surface.

Shoot the No. 3 or No. 4 plane diagonally across the boards from the leading edge to the rear edge. Work your way down along the length of the panel and repeat the process until you've contacted every part of the surface. Then use the No. 4½ plane to clean up the marks left by diagonal planing. Run this plane the full length of the panel, being sure to follow the grain of the wood (you may have to reverse the planing direction if interior boards have an opposing grain direction). Keep the blade sharp to ease your labors. Use the cabinet scraper to clean up any defects. I find that scrapers mounted to an adjustable handle (mine has a ball-and-socket joint) are the easiest and most effective to use.

After scraping, the panel is ready for final sanding. If your scraper was sharp, you should be able to start in with 180-grit sandpaper on an orbital finishing sander capable of holding half a sheet of sandpaper. I recommend Stikit self-adhesive paper made by 3M: It lasts longer than many standard sandpapers and, best of all, it allows you to change the paper in less than 10 seconds. You must, however, replace the base pad on your sander with the inexpensive pad sold by the suppliers of the paper (see Appendix 1).

Lightly dampen the surface of the panel and sand it again, this time using 220-grit paper. For a smoother finish, continue to 320 grit. Stack the surfaced panels with their frames along the east wall to the left of the drill press.

If you opt for the belt sander, start with 80 grit, running the sander back and forth along the length of the boards. Unless you have more than one belt sander, do all the panels at 80 grit

before changing belts to 100 grit and then to 120 grit. Finish the job with the orbital sander. Depending on the manufacturer of the sandpaper, you can probably start at 120 grit and continue through 150, 180 and 220 grit. Work over a downdraft table, if you have one, or at least attach a vacuum hose to the sanders.

The next step is to cut the panels to final width and length and sort them by function: banked drawer faces, framed panels and solid applied panels. After cutting out individual drawer faces from the panel, re-mark the pyramid and module symbol on the back of each face and stack them with the rest of the drawer faces. It's likely that the framed panels and drawer faces will receive some form of edge treatment, so load them onto Larry, wheel them to the area by the table saw and perform this operation with the router mounted under the side extension table. Stack the panels in a free space along the east wall of the shop. Collate panels that are to receive a frame with these components.

If the project calls for solid end panels, they must be specially milled to

allow for shrinkage and expansion once they are attached to a cabinet side; otherwise, the panels will split. I use a sliding dovetail joint for this, attaching the keyway to the case side and running the mating groove across the panel back. The panel is attached with screws from inside the case to the rear of the panel and allowed to "float" on the front end. In the drawing below, the panel rides on two dovetailed keyways secured to the case side with screws. The front edge is buried in a dado in the face frame and can float in and out inconspicuously. (If the cabinets will not receive a face frame, the front edge of applied panels will show. In this case, the dadoes must be stopped before reaching the front edge of the panel.)

Make this joint by first routing two straight-sided dadoes in the back of the applied panel one-half the depth of the stock and ½" wide. Locate the dadoes 6" from the top and bottom edges. Use the back-to-back clamp to guide the router base. After the dado is cut, insert a dovetail bit, set it to the depth of the dado and run it along the dado's length to produce an undercut on one

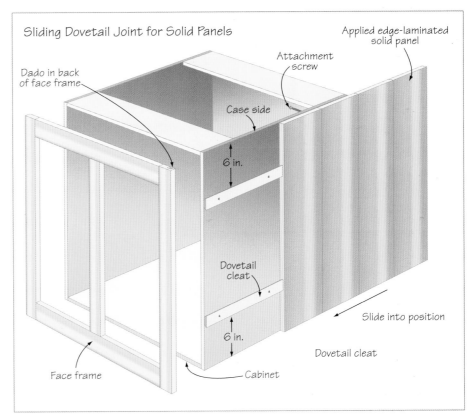

Sliding Dovetail Joint for Solid Panels

Dado in back of face frame

Attachment screw

Applied edge-laminated solid panel

Case side

6 in.

Dovetail cleat

6 in.

Slide into position

Dovetail cleat

Face frame

Cabinet

side. Move the clamp so that a second pass will produce an undercut on the opposite side.

After routing all the applied panels, create the keyway. Transfer the bit from the handheld router to the router at the shaping station. Select a piece of stock the thickness of the widest portion of the dovetailed dado and run it against the bit. (Adjust the fence and the height of the bit on a test piece until the key matches the groove with just enough play to allow movement.) Store the completed panels and keyways by the carcass components along the south wall of the shop to await finishing and carcass assembly.

Preparing the Drawer Faces

Now bring all the drawer faces to the multipurpose platform to drill for the adjustment cams, which attach the face to the box while allowing the face to be moved up to $\frac{3}{16}$" in any direction. This feature allows the alignment of drawer faces to be fine-tuned with surrounding face components such as doors, other drawer faces and trim elements. Make a jig to locate the 20mm holes that must be bored into the back of the drawer faces, as shown below. Except for faces wider than 6", two cams per drawer are sufficient. Note that the jig provides a choice of holes for locating two or four cams per face.

After locating the cams on the backs

of all the drawer faces, bring the stack of faces over to the drill press. Chuck the 20mm bit into the machine and drill a test hole to fix the depth stop. (The cams should be flush to the surface when pounded all the way in.) Proceed to drill the cam holes, centering the brad point of the bit on the pin hole made by the awl. When the process is complete, wheel the stack over to the shaping station if a molded edge is needed.

Finish-sand the faces the same way you did the applied side panels. (If these panels were a part of the project, the setup is already in place.) Then stack the faces with the drawer box components.

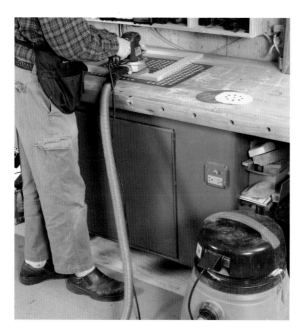

Considering dust the number one enemy to my body (number two is noise), I now use a downdraft table and a trigger-activated vacuum attached directly to the sander whenever possible. Between the suction of the table and the shop vacuum, virtually no dust enters the shop — or my lungs — during sanding operations.

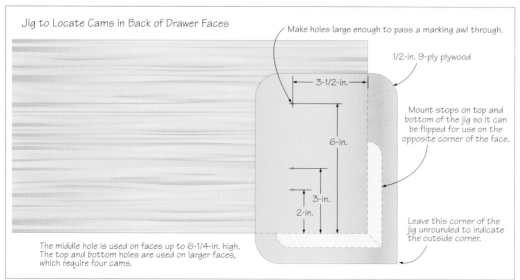

Jig to Locate Cams in Back of Drawer Faces

Make holes large enough to pass a marking awl through.

1/2-in. 9-ply plywood

3-1/2-in.

Mount stops on top and bottom of the jig so it can be flipped for use on the opposite corner of the face.

6-in.

3-in.

2-in.

Leave this corner of the jig unrounded to indicate the outside corner.

The middle hole is used on faces up to 6-1/4-in. high. The top and bottom holes are used on larger faces, which require four cams.

To locate the shank holes in the front of the drawer boxes that attach the adjustment cams fixed in the back of the drawer faces, I place steel centering pins in the holes drilled for the cams. With the drawer slid into its cabinet, I hold the face in its approximate position and press it against the drawer box. In so doing, I make marks where the holes are to be drilled.

Preparing Other Solid Stock Components

Three remaining components get made from the solid stock: the top frames, the side and back supports for slide-out shelves and the exposed nailers. Optional components, such as appliance garages and cubbyhole shelves below upper cabinets, also get processed at this time. The nailers have already been cut to width and length, so find them in the stacks against the east wall and load them up on Moe or Larry. If they need edge treatment, wheel them to the shaping station (for the sake of efficiency, use the same edge shape you applied to the drawer faces). Sand the wood to 180 grit and bring the completed nailers to the stack of carcass components along the south wall of the shop.

The design I use for slide-out shelves requires that two wood sides, a front and a back be joined to a bottom of ³⁄₄"-thick hardwood plywood; bring these components to the work area from the south wall. The joinery is accomplished with spline biscuits and finish nails. Standardize the procedure by

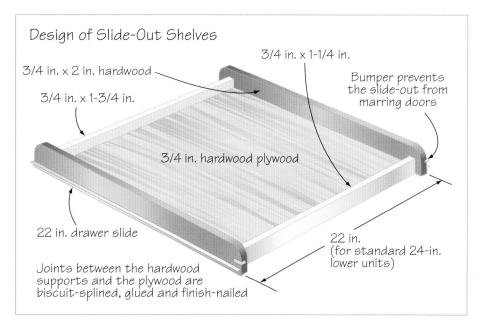

Design of Slide-Out Shelves

3/4 in. x 2 in. hardwood

3/4 in. x 1-3/4 in.

3/4 in. x 1-1/4 in.

Bumper prevents the slide-out from marring doors

3/4 in. hardwood plywood

22 in. drawer slide

22 in. (for standard 24-in. lower units)

Joints between the hardwood supports and the plywood are biscuit-splined, glued and finish-nailed

using a stick marked with the slot centers for the spline biscuits; use one face of the stick for laying out the sides and the other for the fronts and backs. Transfer the marks to the components, including the ³⁄₄"-thick shelf bottoms, and make the slots. Hold the material securely against the multipurpose platform; clamp a 2×4 across the platform for a backstop. I like to round the front edges of the side supports and break all the edges with a ³⁄₁₆" roundover bit. Sand the stock to 220 grit. Collate all the components into their individual units and stack them against the south wall.

Now bring the top frames to the platform and separate the sides from the fronts and backs. Prepare the stock for the spline biscuits using the same jig designed for the splining of the door frames. When slotting is complete, resort the components into their individual units but don't bother to stack them along a wall. It's time for the next major production block — component assembly — and the top frames might as well be the first project.

A slide-out shelf in operation: Note that the door is on hinges that carry it out of the way of the slide-out.

11 | assemble the components

The component-assembly production block serves to clean up all the loose ends that have been proliferating in the shop. Carcass top frames and face frames are assembled, along with doors, panels, drawers and sliding shelves. In addition, edge-banding is applied to any sheet stock components that require it. All the assembled components are sanded in preparation for finishing, thereby avoiding the need for disruptive sanding operations during that production block. After finishing, all that remains in the construction phase of the project is assembly of cases and installation of the components.

Panels and Frames

Bring all the panels and frame bundles up to the platform from their holding area to the left of the drill press. Untape a set of frames and find the corresponding panel or panels. Set up the pipe clamp support (if it's not up already), dry fit the panel and continue dry fitting units until you run out of room. Glue each unit, taking great care to keep the joints flush along the edges, and the panel perfectly square. Use a 12" square against the inside edge of the frame and, if the clamps allow enough clearance, check the diagonals for squareness. If the panels are solid wood, rub paraffin from a candle onto the corners to prevent the glue from cementing the panels to the frame. (Unless solid panels are allowed to float in their frames, the likelihood of the wood splitting during periods of shrinkage is great.)

Remove the clamps as soon as possible (remember to chalk the clamping time on the units), reclamp a new unit and begin cleanup by scraping off the excess glue. Clean up the joints between rails and stiles with a sharp block plane and cabinet scraper. After all the units have been glued, released and cleaned, wheel them to the shaping station to receive their molded edge treatment. (If, however, you're only going to break the sharp edge with a sharp block plane or a $\frac{1}{8}$" roundover bit in a laminate trimmer, do this on the work platform.) Commence sanding with 150-grit paper on a quarter-sheet orbital sander. Moisten the wood slightly to raise the grain at the 220-grit stage and finish-sand at 320 grit. Stack the completed units against the wall to the left of the drill press to await finishing and hardware installation.

Face Frames

If you have face frames in the project, stack the taped bundles on Larry and roll them to the platform. Open one bundle and lay out its components in the correct configuration. Since the face frame gets screwed together from the back, the components must lie face down on the table. It's tricky at first to picture the layout of a face frame from the perspective of the inside of the cabinet, but you soon get used to it. (If you get confused, face the elevation card away from you and hold it up to a light. You are now looking at the face frame from inside the cabinet.)

Once the components are properly oriented, mark the position of the interior joints. This must be done to careful measurement, unless the components themselves can be used as spacers. (For example, the location of a mid-stile that carries a mid-rail can be determined by sliding the mid-rail first to the top, then to the bottom of the mid-stile, thereby establishing its position to the fixed distance of the mid-rail, as shown in the drawing on page 76.)

Begin the fastening process with the innermost joints of the frame. Spread a little bit of glue on the end of the rail and butt it firmly against its adjoining piece at the marks. Secure the assembly under the vise-grip-type clamp, being sure the head of the clamp bears across the butt joint. In some hardwoods you may have to drill pilot holes for the face-frame screws. Using a 3"- to 4"-long square head bit, drive the fasteners home. If other components are to be joined to the clamped piece, repeat the process. Now release the clamp, lift up the joined components and remove the excess glue with a damp rag. Wipe off the work surface too. Note in the photo on page 76, bottom, that I have installed three Kreg plates with vise-grip-type clamps on my workbench so that I can more easily and quickly get the joints of larger face frames under a clamp for screw joining. Continue until all the frame components have been joined, then check with diagonal measurements to ensure the frame is square. (You may have to clamp a temporary brace across the structure.) Set the assembly aside to dry. Continue until all the units have been assembled, and let the entire batch sit overnight to allow the glue to reach maximum strength.

Component Assembly

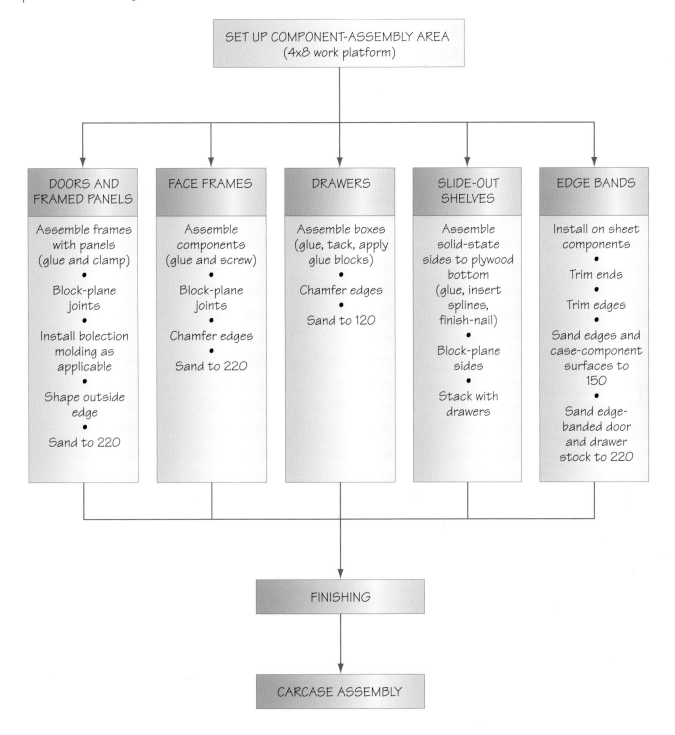

SET UP COMPONENT-ASSEMBLY AREA
(4x8 work platform)

DOORS AND FRAMED PANELS

Assemble frames with panels (glue and clamp)

•

Block-plane joints

•

Install bolection molding as applicable

•

Shape outside edge

•

Sand to 220

FACE FRAMES

Assemble components (glue and screw)

•

Block-plane joints

•

Chamfer edges

•

Sand to 220

DRAWERS

Assemble boxes (glue, tack, apply glue blocks)

•

Chamfer edges

•

Sand to 120

SLIDE-OUT SHELVES

Assemble solid-state sides to plywood bottom (glue, insert splines, finish-nail)

•

Block-plane sides

•

Stack with drawers

EDGE BANDS

Install on sheet components

•

Trim ends

•

Trim edges

•

Sand edges and case-component surfaces to 150

•

Sand edge-banded door and drawer stock to 220

FINISHING

CARCASE ASSEMBLY

Clean up these frames the same way you'd clean other frame construction: Use a block plane on the surfaces and edges of the joints, then use an orbital sander to sand the wood to 320 grit. Break the edges of the wood inside the frame and out with a $\frac{1}{8}$" roundover bit in a laminate trimmer. Set completed frames to the right of the drill press to await finishing and hinge-plate installation.

Immediately after gluing up a frame and panel unit, check it for square by holding a small steel square against the inside edge of the rails and stiles. Make adjustments by lightly tapping the edge with a rubber mallet.

When screwing a face frame together, make sure the pieces stay flush. I use a commercial plate and clamp system to hold the two pieces flush. In my friend's shop (shown here), three such plates and clamps are installed in the work surface so you hardly have to move the face frame to orient a joint under a clamp.

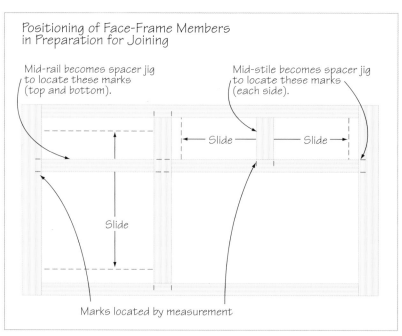

Positioning of Face-Frame Members in Preparation for Joining

Mid-rail becomes spacer jig to locate these marks (top and bottom).

Mid-stile becomes spacer jig to locate these marks (each side).

Slide

Slide

Slide

Marks located by measurement

Drawers

The first step in drawer assembly is to sort the pieces into units. (You don't need the faces at this time.) The sizes of the drawers are listed on the elevation cards. Transfer the module code to the underside of the drawer bottom and stack the units on the work platform, leaving enough room to assemble one unit.

Since the box depends on the squareness of the bottom, double-check this piece with diagonal measurements before assembling each unit; take care of slight discrepancies with a block plane. When you are satisfied, surround each bottom with its box, checking to be sure the joints close completely. Apply glue lightly to both surfaces of the joint, and tack the structure together with $\frac{5}{8}$" slight-headed brads shot from an air-powered tacker. (You can also use staples if you have the gun for them, but they are harder to hide.) Set the box upside down and check for square. Then glue $\frac{1}{4}$" × $\frac{1}{4}$" × 2" softwood glue blocks along the juncture of the bottom with the sides, two to a side, to prevent the boxes from racking. Now put the box in the area where it can sit until the glue has thoroughly dried (in the former area of the feed platform, on a piece of plywood raised up on 12" lifts).

Continue to put finished boxes in the drying area, carefully stacking them upside down, one on top of the other. Wait until the next day to move the boxes back to the platform and break the edges of the plywood with the $\frac{1}{8}$" roundover bit. Return them to the drying area to await installation of hardware and faces. If you used prefinished plywood, you will need to apply finish only at the cut and rounded edges.

The lock rabbet joint is a secure and attractive way to join the walls of a drawer box together.

Glue and a few finish nails (installed with a pneumatic tacker) hold the joint itself together.

Glue blocks are used as additional insurance to hold the boxes square. I use $\frac{5}{8}$" slight-headed brads to hold the blocks in place while the glue dries.

Slide-Out Shelves

Bring the components for the sliding shelves to the multipurpose platform, and sort the solid stock and ¾"-thick plywood bottoms into individual units. Write the module code on the undersides of the shelf bottoms. Begin assembly by inserting the spline biscuits. Then shoot finish nails with your air nailer to hold the front and back to the bottom while the glue sets. Be sure these pieces are flush to the edge of the bottom on each end (use a block plane on them until they are). Install the sides in the same manner. Stockpile the completed units with the drawer boxes.

Edge-Banding

Carcass sides, floors, ceilings, partitions and shelves are edge-banded along only one edge. Doors and drawer faces made of sheet stock are edge-banded along all four edges. Generally, I apply a veneer edging using a heat gun table system (see Appendix 1 for source). Many wood species are available to match the hardwood plywood. Once you get the hang of using the machine, it's relatively fast to do. If you are in a real hurry and you live close to a "real" cabinet shop, you might consider bringing all your components there to be edge-banded by powered edge-banders that apply the banding as fast as you can feed the stock into the conveyor belt.

If you are edge-banding certain components with solid wood, glue on the edge-banding and allow it to dry for several hours. Cut the ends to length (I find using a hand dovetail saw is about as fast as setting up a cutting process on the table saw). I use a router mounted on a commercial base system to trim the sides of the edge-banding flush as shown in the photos on page 79: Sand the edge-bandings to 150 grit and lightly hand sand the edges to break the edge. Now stack these panels against the south wall to await finishing.

Hold out edge-banded door and drawer faces for edge treatment. In my designs, this usually amounts to breaking edges with a ⅛" roundover bit mounted in a laminate trimmer. Sand these components (at least the outside surfaces) all the way up to 320 grit. Store completed components against the wall to the left of the drill press. Door hinges will be installed after finishing. Adjustable cams will be pressed into the backs of the drawer faces and pulls will be installed.

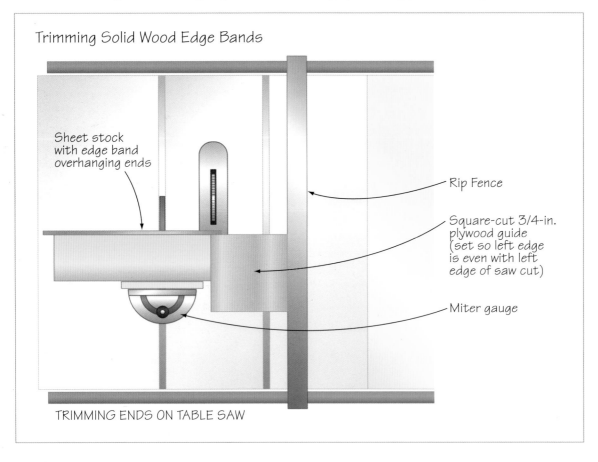

Trimming Solid Wood Edge Bands

Sheet stock with edge band overhanging ends

Rip Fence

Square-cut 3/4-in. plywood guide (set so left edge is even with left edge of saw cut)

Miter gauge

TRIMMING ENDS ON TABLE SAW

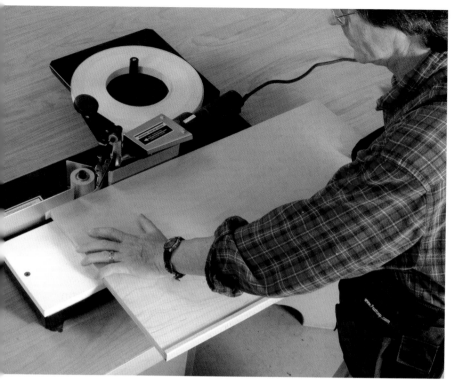

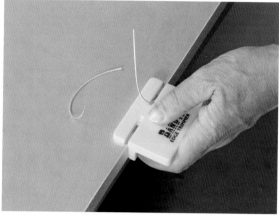

A handheld edger makes quick work of trimming the veneer. I follow up with a soft-pad sanding block fitted with 180-grit paper.

I now use an edge-banding machine to apply veneered edging to panel stock. Once you get the temperature of the gun and the rate of feed right, the tape goes on quickly and stays there. Experiment on scrap until you get it down.

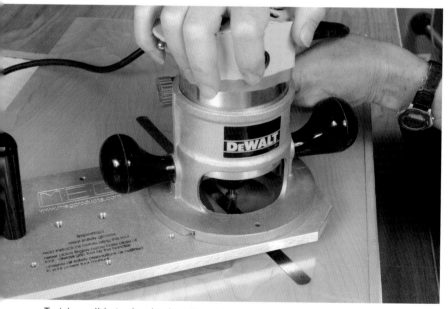

To trim solid stock edge-banding, I use an aftermarket router base system made by MEG Products (see Appendix 1). Here I'm setting the router bit to a feeler gauge to keep the bit a few thousandths of an inch above the surface of the panel to prevent any marring. The edging will protrude slightly after the routing process, but a few passes with an orbital sander will bring it perfectly flush.

Gripping the router and the base, I carefully run the square-cutting bit over the edging.

12 | finish

My cabinetmaking colleagues tell me that I take a rather unique approach to scheduling the finishing of my products. Unlike many small cabinet shops, I finish all the components before final assembly. In fact, I generally use prefinished plywoods that need to be finished only along their banded edges. I remind my colleagues that my methods of building the cabinets are just as un-orthodox as the size and overhead of my shop. I work the way I do in keeping with a basic rule I introduced in section one: No project will be assembled until there is a place outside the shop for it to go. I don't have room for my cabinetwork when it is put together; the last step in my produc-tion process must therefore be the case assembly. After that, the job is out the door.

Finishing Materials

In the past few years, I have made a major shift in the type of finish I apply to my cabinetry, swinging from pene-trating oil finishes to tung oil varnishes to the new, high-quality water-based lacquers and polyurethanes. I'd wanted to use these surface film finishes for a long time because of their great resist-ance to abrasion, heat and water. They dry fast too; the thought of applying a finish to an entire set of kitchen cabi-nets and delivering them the same day was almost too good to be true.

Although I still occasionally have a client who insists on an oil-and-varnish finish (the depth and rich luster of a penetrating finish is, admittedly, unob-tainable with a surface finish), I can usually talk them into a compromise: I apply a slightly thinned spar varnish for the first coat to imbue the wood with that characteristic, lovely amber glow and then — after at least a 24-hour drying period — I apply two to three coats of water-based surface-film finish.

Preparation

Whether using surface-film finishes or penetrating oils, you should prepare the wood and the shop for the applica-tion of the finish. First and foremost, remember that the quality of the finish directly depends on the quality of the surface preparation. This means sand-ing — the finer and more thorough the sanding, the higher the luster of the finish. Follow the suggestions for sand-ing mentioned in the previous chapters, and raise the grain of the wood at least once at the 220-grit stage. (The first application of a water-based finish or sealer will raise the grain again some-what; take care of this by sanding be-tween coats.) When sanding is completed, vacuum the shop thorough-ly and run the dust collector or an ex-haust fan to remove the dust particles from the air. Don't dampen the floor to keep down the dust if you are going to spray water-based lacquer; it doesn't like high humidity and tends to blush (turn white) under these conditions.

Make sure the temperature of the shop is above 65° F before you apply the fin-ish. (Water-based finishes love the dry heat from woodstoves, and, unlike ni-trocellulose-based lacquers, they can be applied in the vicinity of an open flame.) Don't store water-based finishes on the shop floor during the cold months, especially if the floor is a con-crete slab. In fact, be sure to warm the finish to above 65° F before applying it.

I set up the finishing area in the southern half of my shop (as shown in the drawing on page 15) by placing two 8'-long 2×4s across a pair of 32" lifts. I secure the 2×4s to the lifts with drywall screws and run self-adhesive padding (weather stripping works well) along the tops of the 2×4s to protect the components' surfaces. I set blocking on the floor by the west wall to hold the components during intermediate stages of the finishing process.

Finishing Procedures

The basic finishing procedure for all components, regardless of the type of finish used, includes the following steps:

- Check the surface for scratches and remove any with a cabinet scraper. Sand with 320-grit wet/dry sandpaper.
- Apply the finish to all accessible surfaces and set the piece aside to dry along the wall or on a drying rack.
- After the finish dries, reposition the piece to apply finish to the surfaces missed in the previous step.
- Sand the surface lightly with 220-grit sandpaper to remove dust bumps and raised grain.
- Apply a second coat of finish to all surfaces.
- Rub out the second coat with 320-grit wet/dry sandpaper and apply a final coat of finish.
- For the highest sheen, buff out the finish with rubbing compound on a wool pad either by hand or, more effectively, with an electric buffer (such as those sold at auto supply stores).

If the wood is a porous species, such as oak, ash or cherry, use a sanding sealer for the first coat of a surface-film finish. This seals the pores and allows better buildup of the films. Porous woods drink up oil finishes, leaving almost no residual oil on the surface after the first, and sometimes even after the second, coat. (Residual oil must be wiped off the surface after about 15 to 30 minutes, before it becomes tacky.)

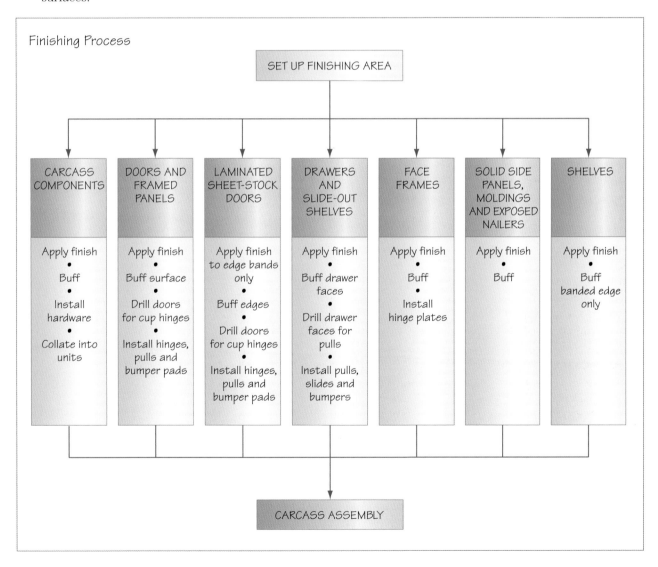

Finishing Process

SET UP FINISHING AREA

CARCASS COMPONENTS	DOORS AND FRAMED PANELS	LAMINATED SHEET-STOCK DOORS	DRAWERS AND SLIDE-OUT SHELVES	FACE FRAMES	SOLID SIDE PANELS, MOLDINGS AND EXPOSED NAILERS	SHELVES
Apply finish • Buff • Install hardware • Collate into units	Apply finish • Buff surface • Drill doors for cup hinges • Install hinges, pulls and bumper pads	Apply finish to edge bands only • Buff edges • Drill doors for cup hinges • Install hinges, pulls and bumper pads	Apply finish • Buff drawer faces • Drill drawer faces for pulls • Install pulls, slides and bumpers	Apply finish • Buff • Install hinge plates	Apply finish • Buff	Apply finish • Buff banded edge only

CARCASS ASSEMBLY

Preparation for Case Assembly

Once finishing is complete, prepare the components to be assembled into cases. Beginning with the carcass components, install the sockets for the adjustable legs onto the floors, and screw the drawer slides and hinge plates into the appropriate holes on partitions and side panels. (Use large-shank "system screws" to attach this hardware to the predrilled 5mm holes.) Before stacking these components against the south wall, collate them into their modules. Include the vinyl-coated back, the stretchers (for lower units), nailers (for upper units and freestanding hutches) and other case components, such as spacers and braces for kitchen accessories (lazy Susans, slide-out baskets, etc.). In each unit, stack the vinyl cabinet backs first so they can act as spacers between the modules.

Now drill the doors for the cup hinges. If you have a drilling and insertion machine for your brand of cup hinges, simply set the right- and left-hand stops to coordinate with the spacing of the hinge plates on the case sides and drill away. The drawing on page 83 shows the details of laying out this spacing. Since this machine also presses the hinges securely into place (they can still be removed by backing out two screws; the plastic inserts to receive them remain pressed into the 5mm holes), the only preparation remaining for the doors is to install the pulls and rubber bumper pads. Use a jig, as shown in the photo at right, bottom, to locate the shank holes for the pulls to speed up the process and to eliminate alignment problems.

You can, of course, drill and install European cup hinges without expensive machinery. Blum makes a simple jig called the Ecodrill (see the photo at right, above) that you clamp to the door at the center line mark for the hinge. Three drill bits are integrated into the Blum jig, all driven (one at a time) by a tork fitting on your hand drill. With the holes drilled, press in the hinge by hand and screw it in place.

The other components requiring hardware are the drawer faces and

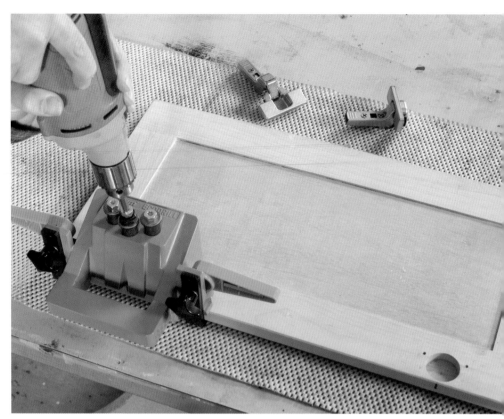

A fixture made by Blum (see Appendix 1) makes it easy to drill the three holes necessary for the installation of a European cup hinge. The fixture, which contains three drill bits, clamps securely to the panel at a center line mark. Simply insert the drive bit into the top of each drill bit to make the sequence of three holes.

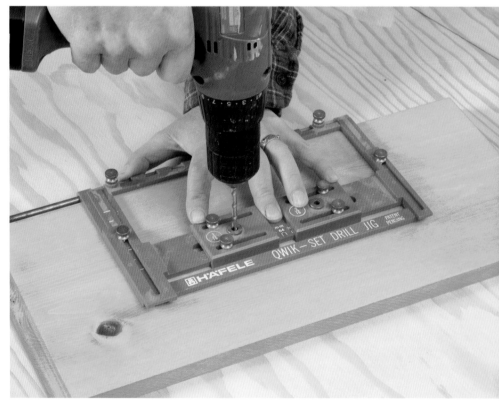

This fixture made by Hafele North America Co. (see Appendix 1) provides perfect alignment and indexing of holes for installing door and drawer pull hardware.

boxes, the sliding shelves and the face frames. Prepare for the hardware by removing the 2×4s from the 32" lifts and setting the multipurpose platform in its place. Begin with the drawer faces. Put them face up on the platform on a piece of soft cloth and drill shank holes for the pull hardware. (Devise your own jig or purchase a commercial model; see Appendix 1. The photo at on page 82 shows the jig made by Hafele North America Co.) Install the pull and set the faces down in the area with the drawer boxes.

Now bring the drawer boxes to the platform and install the drawer slides. Be sure the front edge of the slide is snug against the face before fastening it in place. (A self-centering drill bit is helpful here in locating and drilling the pilot holes for the fasteners.) Install the drawer slides for the sliding shelves at this time, and attach the door bumpers to each front corner. Return the com-

pleted drawers and slides to the north portion of the shop. If you are outfitting some of the drawers with dividers, this would be a good time to do it.

The last components to receive hardware are the face frames, if the project requires them. Bring each frame to the work platform but this time, you'll be relieved to hear, place it right side up. Install the mounting plates for the cup hinges along the edges of the frame in the appropriate location. I recommend using a commercial jig (see Appendix 1) for this purpose because it will have to stand up to a lot of drilling. Be aware that hinge plates come in a variety of sizes; the size you use depends on how far the door overlaps the frame. Hinge plates for different overhangs look very much alike; to make sure you install the right ones, try opening a door after the first pair has been installed.

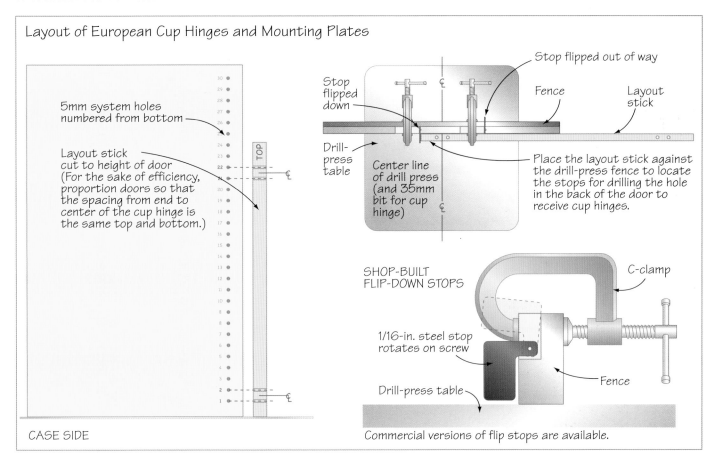

Layout of European Cup Hinges and Mounting Plates

5mm system holes numbered from bottom

Layout stick cut to height of door (For the sake of efficiency, proportion doors so that the spacing from end to center of the cup hinge is the same top and bottom.)

TOP

CASE SIDE

Stop flipped down

Drill-press table

Center line of drill press (and 35mm bit for cup hinge)

Stop flipped out of way

Fence

Layout stick

Place the layout stick against the drill-press fence to locate the stops for drilling the hole in the back of the door to receive cup hinges.

SHOP-BUILT FLIP-DOWN STOPS

C-clamp

1/16-in. steel stop rotates on screw

Drill-press table

Fence

Commercial versions of flip stops are available.

13 | assemble the carcass

The carcass components sit sorted into modules between the assembly platform and the south wall. Put the first unit onto the platform and begin assembly by securing the sides to the floor and top stretchers (or ceiling, if an upper cabinet). Assemble the case face up so you can be sure all the components are flush at their face. Use spline biscuits and drywall screws, or confirmat connectors, to join the pieces. If using the latter, hold the pieces in alignment with pipe or bar clamps while you use the confirmat drill guide and stepped drill (see Appendix 1 for source) to prepare the pilot and shank holes. Once the basic box is together, install partitions, nailers, braces and spacers as called for on the module card.

Now turn the case over and install the back panel. Align it with the outside edge of the floor and staple or screw it in place. Check the case for square with diagonals. When you are satisfied, secure an upper corner of the panel to hold the case square, then drive home the rest of the fasteners. (I usually cut the back $\frac{1}{8}$" smaller than the overall dimensions of the case to prevent it from interfering with the tape measure when taking diagonal measurements.)

If the cabinets have face frames, perform the following four steps: First, check the face of the box for square with diagonal measurements and adjust it accordingly. Second, retrieve the appropriate face frame from the stack to the right of the drill press. Third, roll glue onto the face edges of the case components and set the frame in place. (Check to be sure the position is correct by referring to the module's elevation card, which indicates the amount the face frame overhangs the side components.) Last, secure the face frame to the case with either 6d finish nails or pocket screws driven through the case and into the back of the face frame.

Installing the Other Components

Now's the time for the rest of the parts — side panels, drawers, slide-out shelves, special hardware, moldings and doors — to join with their appropriate cases.

The side panels may be installed in either of two ways, depending on the type of panel. If they are solid wood, connect them to the case with the sliding dovetail described on page 71. Align the keyway on the case by sliding it into its groove on the panel; apply a tiny bead of glue to the keyway where it will contact the case side. (Rub paraffin on the adjacent panel surfaces to prevent them from sticking to the case side in the event glue gets squeezed out.) Position the panel on the case and hold it in place with padded clamps until the glue dries. Note that the panel should fit into a dado cut into the back of an overhanging face frame, or, if there is no frame, it should protrude past the carcass side by the thickness of the door and drawer face stock.

When the glue has set, slide the panel off and fasten the keyway to the case side with slightly countersunk 1" screws. Slide the panel back in place and fix it to the cabinet along its back edge by running in 1¼" screws from inside the case. Don't sink the screws, but cap them with cover caps designed for this purpose (see Appendix 1). Any movement in the panel will now take place at the front edge, which is either buried in a dado or standing free of the case. The back edge, which will be scribed to the wall (or covered with trim molding) during installation, will not move and will thus maintain a perfect fit.

Compared to the previous process, attaching framed panels is simple. Because a framed panel is essentially stable, it's not necessary to provide for shrinkage and expansion. Just position the piece and secure it from inside the case. Be sure the screws attach the frame and not the panels, which must be free to move within the frame. Cover the screw heads with caps.

If the cabinet has a face frame, install the drawer slides now. Use the jig made by the manufacturer of your slides to hold each slide in position while you secure it to the side of the face frame and to the case, as shown at right. If a side or partition is flush to the inside edge of the frame, simply screw the slide to the side or partition. Otherwise, a rear mounting socket catches the back of the slide and is attached to the case back with screws (use only two screws initially, one in the horizontal adjustment slot and one in the vertical). With the drawer slides in place (in faceless cabinets, the slides were installed immediately after the case sides were finished; see chapter twelve), install the drawer boxes.

Now attach the faces to the boxes in the following manner: Insert metal centering pins in the 20mm holes drilled for the adjustment cams (available from the supplier of the cams; see Appendix 1) and hold the face in its intended position on the cabinet. Press the face against the drawer box so that the pins mark the position of the shank holes. Remove the face and drill the shank holes in the front board of the drawer box. Remove the centering pins and tap the adjustment cams into place. (Protect the face during this step with a piece of carpet on the work platform.) Attach the drawer face to the box. When closed, the drawer face should touch the face frame equally on all four sides. If it does not, adjust the position of the slides by either moving the rear mounting brackets along the adjustment slots or moving the rear of the slide up and down along the slotted hole in the slide. If it's necessary to shim the slide-out, use strips of fine sandpaper. When you've achieved a satisfactory fit, secure the brackets by screwing through the holes provided.

Install the slides for the sliding

A specially designed jig made by Hafele North America Co., (see Appendix 1) attaches to the front of a hand drill and guides a drill bit into the corner of a case assembly to create a pilot hole for the Hafele confirmat connection fitting. The drill bit is stepped and tapered to conform to the shape of the fastener. Confirmat fittings are extremely strong and can be drawn in and out of their holes many times without losing fastening power.

The back panel not only helps hold a cabinet case together, it also provides a perfect gauge for making the case square (assuming, of course, the back panel was made square). Tack the two bottom corners to the bottom of the case, then carefully tack along an edge, making sure the panel and the side of the case are flush.

shelves in the same way. Slide the unit into place and check for smooth operation. Check adjustable shelves for fit in their cases — they shouldn't bind along the sides as they travel up and down. Remove these shelves, however, to ship them separately.

At this time, install any special fixtures, such as lazy Susans, slide-out baskets, towel bars or tilt-out trays. Larger items often require the use of special braces to receive mounting hardware. Cut these to fit, and install them with screws. After installation, check all the fixtures for proper operation.

Most moldings are applied to the cabinets after they have been installed, because the moldings generally span more than one module. If, however, a unit has moldings that are integral to it, cut these to fit and install them with finish nails. Fill the holes with a color-matched putty. Sometimes a standard color will be close enough; if not, I mix various putties until I create a good match.

The doors are the last components to be installed in the cases. If all has gone according to plan, the hinge arms will slide right into the mounting plates without a whimper. I'm always amazed when this happens, and it does 99 times out of 100. All that remains is to adjust the hinges until an equal margin of space appears around the perimeter of the door. The ingenuity of these hinges becomes apparent as you realize you are given three planes of adjustment to work with: in and out, side to side and up and down. If the door abuts a drawer face, remember that the face is also adjustable on its inset cams. It does not take long to equalize all the margins. Of course, the slight racking and settling of the carcasses during installation will likely create the need for some final adjustments.

Your last task on the doors is to check that the proper hinge has been used. On certain cabinets (for example, those with slide-out shelves), a wide-angle-type door hinge must be used. This variety of hinge carries the door completely clear of the opening so that slide-outs are unobstructed when ex-

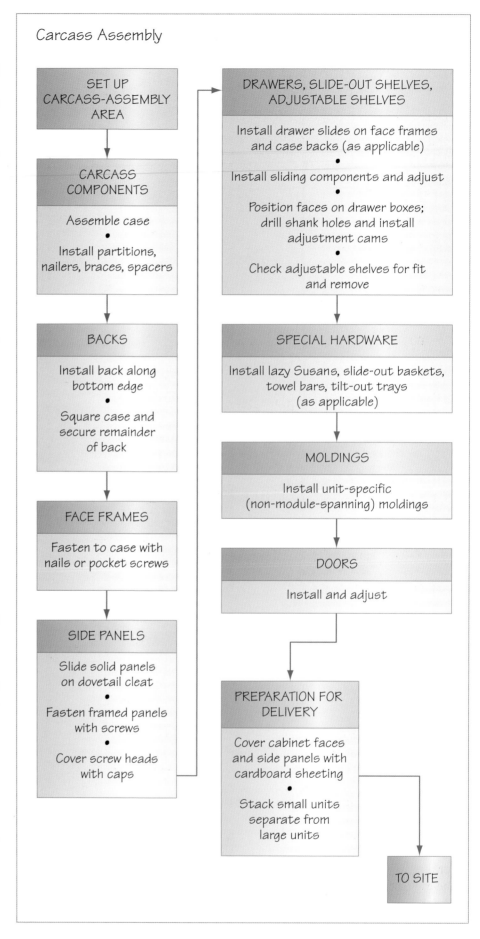

Carcass Assembly

SET UP CARCASS-ASSEMBLY AREA

CARCASS COMPONENTS

Assemble case
•
Install partitions, nailers, braces, spacers

BACKS

Install back along bottom edge
•
Square case and secure remainder of back

FACE FRAMES

Fasten to case with nails or pocket screws

SIDE PANELS

Slide solid panels on dovetail cleat
•
Fasten framed panels with screws
•
Cover screw heads with caps

DRAWERS, SLIDE-OUT SHELVES, ADJUSTABLE SHELVES

Install drawer slides on face frames and case backs (as applicable)
•
Install sliding components and adjust
•
Position faces on drawer boxes; drill shank holes and install adjustment cams
•
Check adjustable shelves for fit and remove

SPECIAL HARDWARE

Install lazy Susans, slide-out baskets, towel bars, tilt-out trays (as applicable)

MOLDINGS

Install unit-specific (non-module-spanning) moldings

DOORS

Install and adjust

PREPARATION FOR DELIVERY

Cover cabinet faces and side panels with cardboard sheeting
•
Stack small units separate from large units

TO SITE

A jig (made by Blum and most other manufacturers of European drawer slides) holds the corner-mounted drawer slide in perfect alignment to the face of the face frame so you can secure it accurately to the side wall of the cabinet.

tended. In other cases, such as when two doors share a partition, the overhang is half the normal amount. It's far better to discover an error in hinge selection while you're in the shop rather than at the job site.

Preparation for Delivery

Before taking the completed cabinet off the assembly platform, prepare it for an uneventful ride to its new home. I buy 4' × 8' sheets of corrugated cardboard from a local paper supply outlet (it's amazingly inexpensive, but don't tell them that) and cut sections of it to cover the faces and finished side panels of the cabinet. The doors and drawers are left installed (except in very large units where their weight becomes a

factor) and are thus secured in place. If you leave the slide-out shelves in place, put chunks of foam or cardboard between them and the back of the door to fix them in place for shipping. Fix the cardboard to the cabinet with packing tape applied with a handled roller.

Lift the "mummified" cabinet off the platform and put it near the door along the west wall of the shop. As cabinets continue to be assembled and stacked, keep the smaller ones separate from the larger ones. You will load the large ones first, so don't bury them under a stack of small ones. If the project is large and promises to overwhelm the shop, try to deliver the cabinets to the site as the job progresses.

14 | install the product

As the time for installation approaches, the specter of disaster invariably rears its ugly head. What if the cabinets don't fit the space? What happens if the moldings don't resolve in that tricky corner? What if the client doesn't like the work? You may never have to look this specter in the eye, if you lay down the foundation of successful projects: through client consultations; checked and double-checked measurements and layout parameters; and carefully designed cabinets that account for variables in the wall, floor and ceiling surfaces to which they are to be attached. For delivery of the cabinets, careful packing ensures they will arrive free of damage, and a thorough checklist ensures that everything needed for installation will be with you at the site.

Delivery and Installation

LOADING OF DELIVERY VEHICLE	SITE PREPARATION	CASE INSTALLATION
Load large units	Unwrap cabinets and bring to area of installation	Remove doors and drawers
•	•	•
Insert small units inside and between larger units	Establish reference line	Install adjustable legs in socket of lower units
•	•	•
Wrap shelves and insert inside cabinets	Establish lines for top of lower units and bottom of upper units	Set corner unit to lines
•	•	•
Bundle moldings	Fix ledger strips for uppers on wall	Level out from wall
•		•
Secure components		Connect adjoining units in run
		•
		Shim cabinets to achieve straight line along front edge
		•
		Secure lower units to wall; scribe end panel to wall as necessary
		•
		Install corner uppers and join adjacent units; scribe end panel to wall as necessary
		•
		Check upper faces for plumb and straight bottom line

The Delivery

When loading the cabinets for delivery, put the large units on the truck first. Smaller units can be placed around (and occasionally inside) them. The larger units can also hold wrapped bundles of adjustable shelves and other loose items. Moldings should be bundled and taped securely together. (Face the good surfaces inward so only the backs of the moldings are exposed.) Pack the cases tightly so things will not jostle around during the ride; fill gaps with cardboard chunks or moving blankets.

Whether you are delivering the cabinets in your own truck or a rented truck, be sure the insurance covers the contents of the vehicle. You can add a one-time rider to your policy to cover the replacement cost of the cabinetry involved in a specific delivery. If you hire a trucking company, read the details of its coverage and be sure to retain your copy of the freight contract and bill of lading, which specifies what you have placed on the truck.

Preparation for Installation

Over the years I have performed scores of installations, and I have yet to make it to the end of one without discovering the need for a tool or piece of hardware that remained behind in the shop. There always seems to be some new wrinkle that demands something I don't have with me. Fortunately (depending on how you look at it), hordes of other tradesmen are usually on the site and can offer the missing item. I have, however, developed an effective checklist that itemizes all the tools, materials and hardware that you should take with you to a typical installation; check off the items as you pack them onto your truck.

Once you're on the site and have brought all the cabinets, tools and materials into the structure, strip off the cardboard wrappings and check for damage. Unless the cabinet has to go back to the shop for repair (usually scratches and minor impact dings, which can be corrected on-site, are the only damage), bring it into the general vicinity of its final home. When you have inspected and distributed all the cabinets, you are ready to begin installation.

COMPONENT INSTALLATION

Install moldings as specified

•

Putty nail holes

•

Reinstall and adjust doors, drawers, slide-out shelves

•

Install shelf clips and adjustable shelves

•

Cut kickboards to length and install

FINAL INSPECTION

Recheck operation and margin lines of doors and drawer faces

•

Touch-up surface scratches where necessary

•

Wipe down surface and vacuum out cabinet interiors

•

Sweep up site

Installation Checklist

Tools

- [ ] Hand truck
- [ ] Air compressor and guns
- [ ] Chop saw and stand
- [ ] Circular saw w/ extra blades
- [ ] Compass saw
- [ ] Double-edge Japanese saw (Ryobi)
- [ ] Hacksaw
- [ ] Jigsaw w/ extra blades
- [ ] Cordless drills and chargers
- [ ] Drills, drivers, hole saws for above
- [ ] Router w/ bit selection
- [ ] Block plane w/ extra blades
- [ ] 13-oz. hammer
- [ ] Tack hammer
- [ ] Nail sets and punch
- [ ] Set of chisels ($\frac{1}{4}$" to $1\frac{1}{2}$")
- [ ] Tape measure
- [ ] Combination screwdriver
- [ ] Pliers
- [ ] Crescent wrench
- [ ] 24" square
- [ ] 12" combination square
- [ ] Bevel gauge
- [ ] Torpedo level
- [ ] 30" level
- [ ] 78" level
- [ ] Water level
- [ ] Plumb bob
- [ ] String with pin hooks
- [ ] Clamps (C- and deep-throat)
- [ ] Scissor jacks and support box
- [ ] Utility knife
- [ ] Pencil scribe
- [ ] Pencils and sharpener
- [ ] Stud finder
- [ ] Work apron
- [ ] Caulk gun
- [ ] Spotlights
- [ ] Extension cords w/ carpenter's vise
- [ ] Vacuum w/ attachments
- [ ] 2' stepladder
- [ ] 5' stepladder

Hardware

- [ ] Adjustable legs (two extra)
- [ ] Kickboard mounting clips
- [ ] Shelf clips
- [ ] Door bumpers
- [ ] Screw covers
- [ ] Extra hinges w/ mounting plates
- [ ] Extra pulls
- [ ] Uninstalled hardware fixtures
- [ ] Drywall screw selection
- [ ] Brad and finish nail selection
- [ ] Oval-head No.10 screws for uppers
- [ ] Lag screws
- [ ] Extra hardware screws

Miscellaneous

- [ ] First-aid kit
- [ ] Dust mask and earplugs
- [ ] Soap and paper towels
- [ ] Dust covers
- [ ] Cotton rags
- [ ] Flashlight
- [ ] Business cards
- [ ] Final bill and job card
- [ ] Plans
- [ ] Calculator
- [ ] Scale rule
- [ ] Drinking water
- [ ] Lunch
- [ ] Radio

Materials

- [ ] Shim stock
- [ ] Colored filler putty
- [ ] Wood plugs for countersinks
- [ ] Masking tape
- [ ] Latex caulk (color-matched)
- [ ] Epoxy
- [ ] Yellow glue
- [ ] 220- to 320-grit sandpaper
- [ ] Touch-up finish material
- [ ] 0000 steel wool
- [ ] Solvent
- [ ] Rubbing compound
- [ ] Molding stock w/ extra lengths
- [ ] Scrap plywood

Reference Lines

Unfortunately, you can never depend on a floor, wall or ceiling to be plumb, level or square to an adjacent surface, even in new construction. (I once saw a floor deviate from level $1\frac{1}{2}$" over the span of 8'.) Thus the first task during installation is to establish a reference line for each run of cabinets.

The fastest and most accurate way to do this is to use a laser level, though a reservoir-type water level also works amazingly well. Without a laser or water level, you will have to make the reference line with a 78" or 96" level. Check that the level is dead on by setting it on a flat surface, shimming up one end till the center bubble reads level and then flipping the level over and taking another reading. The center bubble should read level again; if not, loosen the bubble's set screws and adjust until you can flip the level without producing a deviation. Adjust the other horizontal bubbles to match the corrected one.

Establish the primary reference line somewhere between the upper cabinets and the counter surface (40" is a standard choice). Draw the line itself by connecting marks established with the water or laser level or by using a straightedge. Now measure down from the reference line to the floor at a number of places until you find the high spot of the floor. Standard practice is to set the counter surface 36" above this point. Assuming the reference line resides 39" above the floor at this point, a mark made at 36" will fall 3" shy of the reference line (distance × as shown in the drawing below). Establish the line for the counter height line around the entire kitchen by making marks at this measurement (in this case, 3" below) relative to the reference line and connecting them with a straightedge. Assuming a spacing of 17" between the counter surface and the bottom of the upper cabinets, mark this distance above the counter line everywhere upper cabinets will be installed. Install ledgers at this reference line to support the bottom of the uppers, carefully cutting them to length to match the run of the cabinets.

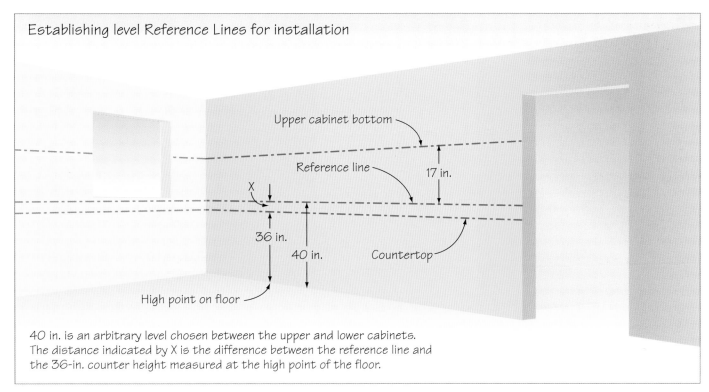

Establishing level Reference Lines for installation

Upper cabinet bottom

Reference line

17 in.

X

36 in.

40 in.

Countertop

High point on floor

40 in. is an arbitrary level chosen between the upper and lower cabinets. The distance indicated by X is the difference between the reference line and the 36-in. counter height measured at the high point of the floor.

Installing the Cabinets

Ready the lower cabinets for installation by removing the drawers and doors and snapping the adjustable legs into their sockets. (Preset the height of the feet to 4", the theoretical standard for producing a 36"-high counter with a $31\frac{1}{4}$" case and $\frac{3}{4}$" of countertop material.) The first cabinet to be installed is usually a corner unit, as it is much easier to work your way out of a corner than into one. The corner unit acts as a fixed point from which the other cabinets begin their runs.

Begin installation by setting the cabinet in its approximate position and bringing the top even with the counter level line (minus the thickness of the counter material). You'll appreciate the ease with which a simple turn of the adjustable legs allows you to do this.

If the corner cabinet is a full-height unit, you will not, of course, have a top corresponding to the counter reference line. In this case, make a mark on the side of the unit at $31\frac{1}{4}$" and use this mark to level the unit with the counter reference line (again, minus counter thickness). Plumb the face of the cabinet, and attach the cabinet to the wall studs with screws run through the nailer in the interior of the cabinet.

Assuming the corner cabinet is a lower unit, lay a level across the cabinet top perpendicular to the wall and check for level, adjusting the front legs as necessary. Next, butt the adjoining cabinets to the corner cabinet and level them to the reference line. Attach them to the corner cabinet along the front edge, making sure the faces are flush. Use screws if there are spacers between the cabinets, or use specially designed connector screws if there are no spacers (see Appendix 1.) Install succeeding cabinets in the run in the same fashion. When all the lower units are leveled and joined along their faces, check the top front edge of the entire run for straightness using either with a stretched string or a long straightedge. Produce a perfect line by adjusting the cabinets in toward and out from the wall; force cedar shims between the cabinets and the walls at the location of

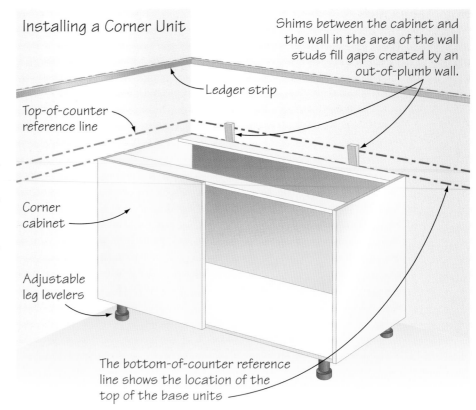

Installing a Corner Unit

Shims between the cabinet and the wall in the area of the wall studs fill gaps created by an out-of-plumb wall.

Ledger strip

Top-of-counter reference line

Corner cabinet

Adjustable leg levelers

The bottom-of-counter reference line shows the location of the top of the base units

studs. When you've achieved a straight run, fasten the cabinets to the wall by running 3" screws at a low angle through the stretcher and into the wall studs. If the last cabinet has an applied panel, scribe it to fit the wall and attach it to the case.

With all the lowers secured, make a temporary countertop by laying scrap plywood over them. The upper units, starting with a corner, can now be set in place on ledgers set to the upper cabinet reference line. Use a cabinet jack to keep them from tipping away from the wall while you check to see if they are sitting plumb and even with adjoining cabinets. Insert shims as necessary. Secure the cabinets to the wall with 3" No. 10 washer-head screws through the exposed nailers in the cabinet. Be sure you hit a stud. If necessary, scribe exposed ends to the walls.

While I hold the applied panel plumb and slightly away from the wall, I scribe the shape of the wall to the edge of the panel for trimming. I've applied a piece of masking tape to the panel to make the line more visible — a standard procedure, especially with dark panels.

After the base cabinets get installed, work on the uppers, beginning with the corner cabinet (if there is one). First, install ledgers to the wall to hold the units to their bottom reference line, and use a specialized cabinet jack (see Appendix 1) to keep the cabinet from tilting forward and to adjust it for plumb. Here I'm installing a shim to bring the base of the cabinet slightly out from the wall.

Install the Components

Start with the various moldings that span the cabinet modules and serve to tie the design together. Cut them to fit with a chop saw on-site and install them with air-driven finish nails. Depending on the design of the cabinetry, you may install pilasters over the spacers between the modules, a plinth along the base of the lower units, a rail onto a nailer between the drawers and doors, a light pelmet under the upper units and a cornice along the top to tie the cabinets to the ceiling. Fill nail holes with matching putty.

Reinstall the doors, drawers and slide-out shelves. Make final adjustments in the hardware to align and even out all the margins. Insert shelf clips into the 32mm-system holes and set the adjustable shelves in place.

Install the kickboards last. As with the moldings, cut them to fit with the chop saw. Use butt joints where they adjoin or intersect. Only the exposed end of a facing board is mitered (and returned to itself), as shown below. Attach the kickboards to the adjustable legs with clips designed for this purpose. Since the clips fit anywhere along the groove provided for them along the kickboard's length, you can hold the board in its approximate position and mark the center of the legs. Then press the clips into place (the clips also slide on their mounts, so perfect alignment is unnecessary) and snap the kickboard into place.

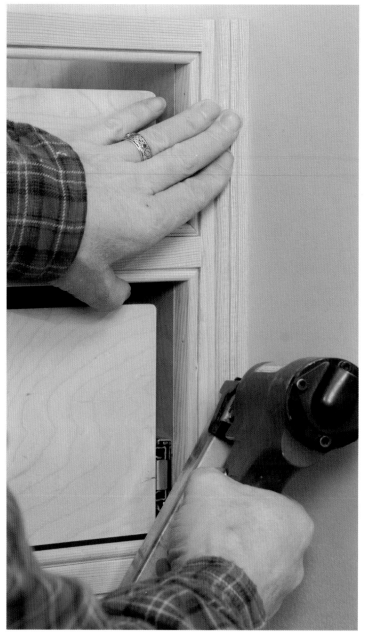

To clean up the joint where the end of a face frame abuts a wall, cover the gap (or potential gap, should shrinkage occur) with a molding.

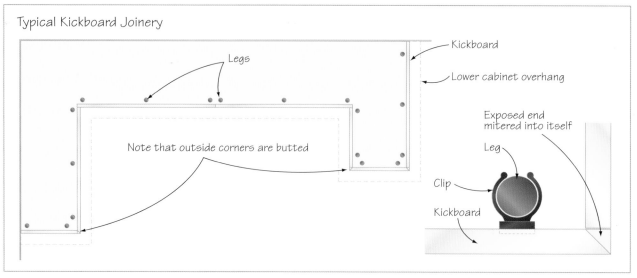

Typical Kickboard Joinery

Legs

Kickboard

Lower cabinet overhang

Note that outside corners are butted

Exposed end mitered into itself

Leg

Clip

Kickboard

Final Inspection

Installation is not complete until you thoroughly inspect the cabinets. Check the operation of all the doors, drawers and sliding shelves. There should be no binding or sagging, and the margins should be as equal as you can get them. Be sure none of the bumpers are missing. If you run into a door that is warped so badly that hinge adjustments aren't enough to hold the door against the face equally at the top and bottom, try adding another hinge to add more force to the closing action. If this does not do it, you may have to build another door. Always cut enough extra door stock to cover such a contingency.

Other things to look for include scratches in the finish and unputtied nail holes. Fill the latter. Sand the former with 320-grit wet/dry sandpaper or 0000 steel wool; touch up with the finish material (either oil applied with a rag or film spread with a small brush). Complete the inspection by running a soft rag over all the exposed surfaces to remove dirt and handprints. Finally, vacuum out the interiors of all the cabinets, including the drawers.

After picking up all the scrap wood, candy wrappers and empty coffee cups, load all your tools and surplus materials into your truck. Go back into the site and sweep up the rooms where you were working. The only thing you should leave behind is a beautiful set of professionally installed cabinets — and maybe a personal touch or two, as discussed in the next section.

Cut removable kickboards to length on-site, then snap them into place on the plastic legs that level and support the base cabinets.

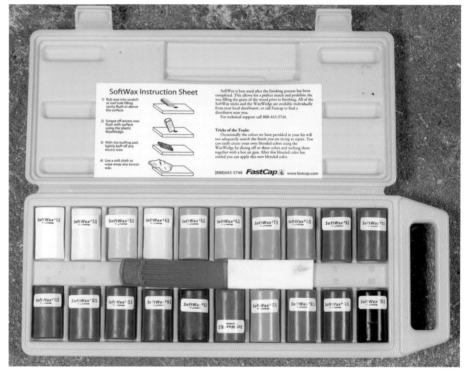

I use this set of wax sticks (see Appendix 1) to fill tack holes. If I can't find a color match, I simply shave the wax of several sticks into a metal cup and melt them together with a heat gun to create the needed hue.

the **business** of cabinetmaking

YOU WILL PROBABLY FIND THAT SETTING UP the workshop is one of the more enjoyable aspects of the woodworking vocation. Cabinetmakers seem to have boundless energy and enthusiasm when it comes to finding the right space in the right location, adjusting the tools and fixtures to be just so and fine-tuning the production process until everything meshes together as one well-oiled cabinetmaking machine. Unfortunately, these activities do not a business make. Having created the machine, it is also necessary to run it; you have to establish a business and find work. For many cabinetmakers, accustomed as they are to shaping things with their hands, this is the biggest challenge of all.

At the outset, you must decide just what you expect to get out of cabinetmaking and where you wish to go with it. There is a big difference between the avocation of working with wood and the occupation of woodworking. When you ask people to pay for your work, you must define the shop as a legal entity. You must procure all the necessary business permits and licenses, and you must register with the Internal Revenue Service (IRS). Financial records must be carefully maintained to satisfy the bureaucrats and to benefit you. Written contracts should be sound for the sake of all parties involved.

Next the goal is to get the business to generate work for itself. You must provide a product or service that enough consumers wish to purchase for a price they are willing to pay. Thus one of your most necessary, and likely most difficult, jobs will be to define your market: who they are, where they are, what they like to buy and how much they can and will spend. As if that were not enough, you will have to learn how to draw a modest but steady portion of that market to your product.

Once you've carved out your niche, it becomes critically important to foster the growth of a good reputation. Contrary to advertising propaganda,

this precious commodity cannot be created by words alone. Only by working harmoniously with clients and trade professionals and by honoring all guarantees of craftsmanship (both written and implied) will your name become synonymous with honesty and quality. If you have a name like that, the world will indeed beat a path to your door.

For many woodworkers, all this might seem too tall an order, but be assured that you already have the raw materials necessary to become a successful businessperson. In creating that well-oiled cabinetmaking machine, you have engaged in forethought and planning, paid painstaking attention to minute details and experienced a deeply rooted desire to produce the best results with only the necessary effort. If the one-third of your being that will act as the businessperson continues to make use of these attributes, the two-thirds of you that anxiously waits to work in the shop will be kept busy indefinitely.

A desk tucked into one corner of my shop serves as a mini office where I can make phone calls, look up hardware and refer to job papers and drawings.

15 | structure the business

The three types of legal business entities a cabinetmaker can choose from are sole proprietorship, partnership or incorporation. Small businesses often start out as sole proprietorships because that's the easiest entity to set up and maintain: The cabinetmaker works alone, receives all the profits (and, of course, assumes all the liabilities) and has the right to sell or terminate the business at will.

Entering into a partnership or incorporating is usually considered in response to a perceived need to grow. While the temptation to do so is very great from the standpoint of profit, growth usually entails certain sacrifices. The mere act of taking on employees, for example, can quickly transform a formerly independent woodworker into a wood monger and an administrator whose primary responsibility is managing people rather than projects. There are other complications. Any employee will have to increase shop profit to the point where you can afford to pay a decent wage plus an additional 30 percent for workmen's compensation insurance, federal unemployment tax, your share of the Social Security and Medicare taxes and an increase in liability-insurance premium. Remember that paying these bills, filing quarterly statements, preparing payroll ledgers every pay period and managing the employee gets done on your own time — or someone else's time that you must pay for. Finally, if you hire one or more employees, you must run your shop in accordance with the equipment and safety standards formulated by the Occupational Safety & Health Administration (OSHA) or risk a substantial fine.

Forming a general partnership brings another worker onto the shop floor without the complications and expense of becoming an employer. Working with another person on an equal basis is often a real shot in the arm, bringing in a burst of creative energy, new ideas and perhaps a larger clientele. Before you say "howdy, partner," consider some of the disadvantages. Working productively with another person means learning to get along together, not always an easy task. Decisions concerning design and production routines become negotiable, and the products of the shop will no longer represent your talents alone. In a general partnership, you are legally liable for all of the work and services of the shop. If your partner produces a lemon and a client responds with sour grapes, both you and your partner must eat the loss.

Although there is no legal way to limit the sharing of liability, you should draw up a written agreement that at least clearly defines the relationship between the partners. In addition to defining the responsibilities of each partner, the agreement should stipulate how income will be drawn from the business, how profits will be shared, the amount of capital to be invested by each partner and the way in which the business may be sold (including buy-sell provisions within the partnership). Neglecting to address these issues in advance can lead to a long, bitter round of negotiations later, which may be impossible to resolve without fattening the wallets of several lawyers.

Because of the increased liability, partners often opt for corporations. (Sole proprietors may incorporate to protect their personal assets from business-related liabilities.) In a corporation, an individual's personal liability is limited to the amount paid for his or her share of the stock. Corporations also offer distinct tax advantages, such as the ability to fully deduct the cost of life and health insurance. (These deductions currently are not available to unincorporated businesses.) A subchapter S corporation is specifically tailored to small businesses: Because shareholders can claim profits, called dividends, as ordinary income, double taxation is avoided. Be aware that a corporation is expensive to set up and maintain, and the reams of paperwork require professional expertise.

In the creation of any business, it makes good sense to seek the advice of qualified professionals. While some lawyers specialize in business law, you can also work with a certified public accountant (CPA). CPAs are usually less expensive than lawyers and often more receptive to small-scale business matters. Find a good CPA by asking other small shop owners for recommendations. An accountant should help you set up the books unless you have expertise in this area.

License, Registration and Reporting Requirements

Most counties and municipalities require businesses that operate within their borders to be licensed. If you operate under a name other than your own, you will probably have to file for a "doing business as" (dba) or "fictitious name" designation. Obtain information on these requirements from city hall or the clerk at the county courthouse.

Your state probably requires registration of a business, especially if the government collects sales tax on the exchange or sale of tangible property (like cabinets). The state will issue a permit to sell taxable property, which also allows you to purchase raw materials and supplies tax-free. (Most wholesalers require tax-exempt customers to file their permit numbers with them.) In addition, your state may require you to register as an employer if you qualify as such. In either case, the state will require you to file quarterly income reports. Obtain state registration information from the taxation agencies located in the capital or from branch offices located in the larger municipalities. Check the Internet and the government section of the phone book.

Last, but far from least, consider the federal government, which will insist on knowing all about your little business. If you run a simple sole proprietorship without employees, your Social Security number serves as identification; otherwise, you are required to file for a Federal Employer Identification Number (FEIN). If you have no employees, your contact with Uncle Sam will be simplified. Any profit from the business is treated simply as income (which is summarized on Schedule C: Profit or Loss From Business) on your personal income tax return. Social Security tax is collected as a self-employment tax, computed on Schedule SE: Self-Employment Tax and filed with your Form 1040. The government requires quarterly payments against your tax liability if it exceeds a certain level.

If you have employees, you will be in touch with the government on a regular basis, depositing federal unemployment tax, Social Security and Medicare taxes and withholding tax, and filing quarterly earnings statements. A corporation must renew its license in the state of registration on a yearly basis and file its own tax returns. (This is the extra paperwork I warned you about.)

Help Without Hiring

If you find yourself sharing the work with another cabinetmaker in your shop, legally you have to hire him or her outright or form a general partnership. You have some ways to get help in the shop without becoming an employer. There is nothing illegal about someone working there without pay (excluding minors, of course). This someone will be either crazy or your spouse (or, more than likely, both). With a spouse's help, the business will generate more income without the headache of additional tax liability and paperwork. There may even be some tax advantages in hiring a spouse, including the ability to create a 401(k) that can shelter a great deal of pretax money. (These laws are constantly changing, so consult an accountant before you decide.)

The other strategy, which I occasionally use when faced with impending deadlines, is hiring subcontractors. The federal government defines subcontractors as people in business for themselves who sell their services to you. A subcontractor can supply you with components, such as drawers and doors, or perform special milling operations, such as running molding or sizing panels, and simply bill you for the work. (If your annual payments to any one subcontractor exceed a certain amount, you will have to file a Form 1099 on the subcontractor at tax time.) As long as subcontractors work on their own time, in their own way (not subject to your management) and on their own equipment, the federal government will not classify them as employees. If you have any questions about the specifics of this relationship, ask the IRS before they ask you.

Set Up and Keep the Books

You cannot successfully run a business of any kind, size or structure without accurately keeping track of what is coming into it and what is going out. Actually, there is no choice: The federal government requires that books be kept for any operating business. Once properly set up, however, the books for a one-person shop are not that difficult or time consuming (perhaps six hours a month) to keep. Well-maintained books are a good barometer of just how well business is doing.

It's a good idea to have professional help for setting up the record-keeping system and even maintaining it. An experienced bookkeeper can generally do as good a job at the books as a CPA and be less expensive. Get recommendations from owners of small businesses in your area: The more an accountant knows about small business, the more he or she can do for you.

Even with the help of a good accountant, the cabinetmaker will still be involved in the day-to-day bookkeeping. Since few accountants enjoy visits from clients bearing a shoe box full of receipts and check stubs, you should find a good way to keep track of daily business. Standard procedure is to post income on an income ledger and outgo on an expenditure ledger. Summarize the entries each month and at year-end simply enter the sum of the monthly subtotals on your tax returns. While standardized ledger forms are available at any office supply store, my versions shown on pages 100 and 101 are specifically tailored for the independent cabinetmaking shop. When using these ledgers, post entries on a regular basis as receipts won't pile up and cause confusion.

The system of bookkeeping I use is single entry cash-basis accounting. Single entry means that income and expenditures are recorded without consideration of other assets or liabilities. Cash-basis accounting is simply recording income when it is received and expenses when they are paid; no provision is made to account for money owed to suppliers or due from customers. To make entries easier, use a checking ledger that lists the same distribution columns that appear in your bookkeeping system. Although these simple accounting practices limit the extent to which the overall health of the business may be assessed at any given point in time, they are sufficient for businesses with a low sales volume,

Month of:

DATE	PROJECT NAME	AMOUNT RECEIVED			
		Deposit Final	TAX COLLECTED	
1				
2				
3				
4				
5				
6				
7				
8				
9				
10				
11				
12				
13				
14				
15				
16				
17				
18				
19				
20				
21				
22				
23				
24				
25				
26				
27				
28				
29				
30				
31				
TOTAL				

EXPENDITURE LEDGER   Month of:

DATE	CHECK NO.	PAYEE	TOTAL AMOUNT	DISTRIBUTION																			
				Materials and Shop Supplies	Shop Rent	Utilities (Including Telephone)	Taxes and Licenses	Subcontractors	Advertising and Portfolio	Bank charges	Vehicle Expenses	Dues and Publications	Freight	Insurance	Laundry	Bookkeeping and Legal Services	Office Expenses	Shop Repairs	Misc. Hand Tools and Bits	Sharpening	Work Clothes	Misc. Costs	Cash (Nondeductible)
1																							
2																							
3																							
4																							
5																							
6																							
7																							
8																							
9																							
10																							
11																							
12																							
13																							
14																							
15																							
16																							
17																							
18																							
19																							
20																							
21																							
22																							
23																							
24																							
25																							
26																							
27																							
28																							
29																							
30																							
31																							
END OF MONTH SUBTOTALS																							
Nondeductible																							

a minimum of uncommitted inventory and a low credit load: a good description of a one-person cabinetmaking shop.

If, however, you plan to hire personnel, prepare to deal with considerably more paperwork and the more complex accounting methods of double entry and accrual basis. As an employer, you will also need payroll ledgers and the complete set of federal and state tax forms.

Finally, two other important aspects of record keeping are equipment depreciation and inventory control. Work with your accountant to design the depreciation schedule and inventory control list most suitable to your specific needs.

Banking

Before you pay a single bill or a single check is accepted, open a separate bank account specifically for business use. The only nonbusiness use of this account may be the occasional withdrawal of cash for personal use (listed in accounting records as a nondeductible expense).

Many banks charge considerably higher service fees for business accounts than for personal accounts, but you don't need to open a business account unless you work under an assumed name (the dba designation). Just open another personal checking account and use it strictly for the shop. If the local commercial banks won't go for that, try a savings bank or a credit union. These customer-owned institutions usually don't charge extra for business accounts, and many don't charge for checks at all.

Immediately deposit all received income in the shop account. When writing checks, always write in the check register and on the check itself the category from the expenditure ledger to which the check's recipient belongs. At least weekly, transfer the numbers from the check register to the monthly expenditure ledger. In this simple system of cash-basis accounting, the income and expenditure ledgers should reconcile exactly with the check register. Any error is usually due to a slip in the

recording of entries (or to faulty arithmetic). An hour or two at the end of each month should allow you to keep everything up to date and your accountant underemployed.

A word about collected sales tax: Bank it, don't spend it! I have a separate savings account (under the same number as my business checking account) that I use solely to park collected sales tax. This way, it doesn't show up as "income" in my regular account and risk being inadvertently (or not so inadvertently) spent. When it's time to pay the tax man, it's always a relief to know that the money is sitting in the account ready to go.

Contracts

A handshake is fine when greeting potential customers, but it's not the way to seal a deal. If a customer wants something from you, get it in writing; that's the only handshake that counts. Unless you have a client's signature (two signatures if you contract with a married couple) on a document that specifies exactly what you promise to supply and for what price, you will have no recourse if the client decides not to pay you for your work. You could end up owning someone else's custom cabinets (not always such a bad thing but not your goal).

Run your business with the hard and fast rule that no work will be performed and no materials will be purchased unless you receive a signed quotation from the customer. (When the quotation form is signed by all the parties involved, it becomes the contract for the specified work.) In custom work a substantial deposit (enough to cover materials) should accompany the accepted quotation. This way, you have some protection even in a worst-case scenario, such as the sudden death of the client. The quotation form I've used for nearly 20 years is available at most print shops or office supply stores; the print shop adds my letterhead at the top, but otherwise the form is unchanged. Buy a two-part carbonless form. For each quotation, keep the copy and give the customer the original.

When filling out the form, accurately record the full name and billing address of the customer and the address of the site for product delivery. Note the phone numbers and e-mail addresses for the customer's office, home and site (if different), and double-check them for accuracy. If a general contractor is involved in the project and the cabinetry is included in that contract, submit the quotation to the contractor. (Since the contractor adds a certain percentage to the bid, it isn't ethical for you to tell the customer the quoted amount.) If the cabinetry has been omitted from the general contract so that the customer can shop and contract for it independently, submit the quote to the customer directly. If you're not certain how matters stand, ask.

The main body of the quotation form is for the precise description of the product. Include the grade as well as the type of materials that will be used, the style of the product (referenced to a sample number if possible), specific sizes and configurations and the type of finish. Be careful not to infer the inclusion of items or processes that are not quoted, such as counter surfaces and their installation. If there is not enough room on the form, don't condense the descriptions; instead, use another sheet and cross-reference it. Have the customer initial your copy of the additional specification sheet.

Immediately below the product description, present the bid itself. (See page 109 for information on pricing.) As in issuing a check, write out the amount in full. If your state has a sales tax, specify "plus tax" after the amount. I generally avoid including sales tax in a bid because it is too easy for a client to perceive my bid as high in comparison with others where sales tax is not quantified. The payment schedule is up to you and the client. I usually ask for one-third down on acceptance of the quotation, a second one-third halfway through the project and the final one-third on delivery. Avoid specifying the date of delivery in the contract if possible. Since delivery can mean different things to different people, specify whether the cabinets are f.o.b. (free on board, i.e., loaded on a truck) your shop or freight paid (delivered to the site).

Acknowledge the receipt of a client's check with a standard receipt form, as shown below. I use a Rediform version, which provides two extra copies. I put one in the client's file, which also contains my copy of the contract, and the other with my income ledger. Note that this type of receipt also provides a space to show the amount of the account and the balance due. This eliminates the need for a separate invoice form to keep track of the account. Look for the form at your local office supply store.

Note that installation is a separate matter entirely. In some states, you must be a licensed subcontractor to perform any work outside your shop. Other states have specified limits. If you intend to do installations (and you probably will, to ensure the best results), check with your state's labor department or contractor's licensing board to see what is required. In any case, it is never wise to include installation within the terms of the original quotation. Installation of custom cabinetry is notorious for unpredictability and labor overruns. The contract for installation should be negotiated, if at all possible, on a cost-plus basis.

A cost-plus contract can take a variety of forms, so specify to the client which of them you mean. One standard version is to charge the cost of labor plus a 10 percent markup on materials. Another method groups labor and materials and adds a specified rate of profit. Sometimes a customer will ask that a ceiling be placed on the contract price. In this case, you're probably better off going with a fixed bid at the top end of your personal estimate. I try to avoid ceilings as I usually find myself working on top of them — without pay of course.

You may need to write into the quotation specific clauses, sometimes referred to as jump-out clauses, to protect yourself from legitimate contingencies. The generic quotation form al-

Quotation Form

Quotation

INTERWOOD

Jim Tolpin
P.O. Box 62
Ferndale, CA 95536

residential - commercial - marine
interior woodworking

SUBMITTED TO	PHONE	DATE
STREET	JOB NAME	
CITY, STATE AND ZIP CODE	JOB LOCATION	
		JOB PHONE

We hereby submit specifications and estimates for:

We Propose hereby to furnish material and labor, complete in accordance with above specifications, for the sum of:

_____ dollars ($_____).

Payment to be made as follows:

All material is guaranteed to be as specified. All work to be completed in a workmanlike manner according to standard practices. Any alteration or deviation from above specifications involving extra costs will be executed only upon written orders, and will become an extra charge over and above the estimate. All agreements contingent upon strikes, accidents or delays beyond our control. Owner to carry fire, tornado and other necessary insurance. Our workers are fully covered by Workmen's Compensation Insurance.

Authorized Signature

Note: This may be withdrawn by us if not accepted within _____ days.

Acceptance of Quotation - The above prices, specifications and conditions are satisfactory and are hereby accepted. You are authorized to do the work as specified. Payment will be made as outlined above.

Date of Acceptance:_____

Signature_____

Signature_____

Receipt Form

RECEIPT   DATE_____ 20____   **No.** 3100

RECEIVED FROM _____

ADDRESS _____

DOLLARS $ _____

FOR _____

ACCOUNT		HOW PAID	
AMT. OF ACCOUNT		CASH	
AMT. PAID		CHECK	
BALANCE DUE		MONEY ORDER	

BY _____

ready lists a number of these clauses: the requirement of a written order to initiate any change in the quoted specifications, freedom from liability due to delays beyond your control and the requirement of the customer to carry his own site insurance. Other contingencies, if predicted, should be covered in a separate clause. These may include the right to substitute materials if the specified materials are unavailable or would unduly delay the project, the right to change the quoted price due to the substitution of items at the client's request and the exemption of liability if the client supplies or requests unconventional or unknown materials (particularly finishing products). In general, if you can foresee the possibility of any contingency that will affect your control over the final product, get it down in writing. If you should think of one after the contract has been signed, write it on all copies and have the client initial it.

The signed quotation form (now a contract) offers a basic guarantee to the purchaser: The product you supply will be the one specified and will be constructed in a workmanlike manner according to standard practices. If you wish to add to this rather nebulous promise, that is entirely up to you. A time frame within which any defects in workmanship will be corrected without charge can be stipulated in writing, but I find it better to leave this unwritten and open. It seems to me that specifying a 30-, 60- or 90-day limit implies that the work will fall apart one day after that time period.

Finally, be sure that your quotation, once accepted, is complete. If the client accepts your bid with the specified deposit and a hearty handshake, you still do not have a contract. Look at the bottom line, the one provided for the client's signature. That signature makes the document legal and binding; don't do business without it. If the unthinkable should occur and the client reneges on subsequent payments, the terms of the contract ensure that the products belong to you and can be liquidated to cover your investment in

them. If, however, you slipped up and delivered the cabinets without taking the final payment, your only recourse may be to place a mechanic's lien on the client's property and take him or her to small-claims court. Consult an attorney, or do it yourself after reading up on it (see Appendix 2).

Insurance

Unfortunately, innumerable things beyond our control besides a client's disinclination to pay a bill are beyond our control. Fortunately, in this country we have a booming insurance industry in this country ready and willing (for a price, of course) to protect us from the vagaries of nature and the inhumanity of man. To protect business and personal assets, cabinetmakers need to purchase two basic forms of business insurance: loss insurance and liability insurance. If the shop has employees, workmen's compensation and disability insurances must also be obtained. Consult your state's labor board to ascertain from whom this coverage gets purchased and the amounts required.

Protection against loss due to fire is provided in a three-part package: "Basic" insures your equipment, inventory and the building, if you own it; "legal liability" covers a rented building and is necessary if your landlord won't include a "hold harmless" clause in your rental agreement; and "property damage" insures other sections of the building not occupied by the business. Optional extended coverage protects against loss from causes other than fire, such as smoke, storms, explosions, vandalism and theft. The premiums for these policies are relatively high for woodworking businesses but can be reduced somewhat by installing dust collection and sprinkler systems and by using nonflammable finishing materials.

Liability insurance offers protection from lawsuits in the event that a nonemployee sustains an injury while in your shop. (Have you ever watched helplessly as a curious customer picked up a gleaming 2" chisel, said "This looks sharp," and proceeded to slice off a chunk of thumb?) Of course, liability

insurance also protects customers if they should suffer from any ineptitude on your part (for example, when you show a client how sharp the chisel is by slicing off the end of his or her thumb). "Product liability," sometimes called "works completed" coverage, covers you in the event that your product, once beyond the shop's doors, somehow manages to injure somebody or cause damage. Don't laugh: I once had a lazy Susan go berserk, literally flying off her hinges and strewing $75 worth of exotic spices across my client's kitchen floor. If someone had slipped on them, it wouldn't have been something to sneeze at. Liability premiums depend on the amount of coverage desired, the projected gross annual income and the number of employees retained. Since I have no employees and do not operate as a subcontractor (I am considered a vendor), I have not had to buy workmen's compensation or disability insurance. In addition to a basic package of loss and liability insurance, I purchase my own medical coverage. To keep the rate on the latter down, I accept a large initial deductible.

For all these insurances, select a broker who has experience insuring woodworking shops. A knowledgeable broker can help determine the amount of coverage you need and clarify the details of the coverage as they relate to the woodworking business. Stay away from brokers without commercial experience because they will not know how to specify the details of your operation or ask the right questions to obtain the lowest premium rates.

16 | market analysis, product design and pricing

The business of the custom cabinetmaker is to supply people with cabinetry designed to meet specific needs. These needs can range from the purely aesthetic to the strictly pragmatic. To become a viable part of this marketplace, cabinetmakers must learn who the clients are and how to find them and develop appealing products that can be built efficiently. Cabinetmakers must learn to price this work to ensure not only survival but profitability within a few years. Otherwise, this work won't rise beyond a hobby — and I mean that literally from the IRS's point of view.

The Clientele

The survival of the custom cabinetmaking business attests to the existence of aware, appreciative consumers, but this clientele is neither evenly distributed across the country nor homogeneous in character. It is easy to assume that the patrons of the custom shop come from the upper-income levels of the population, but I have discovered that there is considerably more to the demographics of our clientele than money. Although I can't claim statistical accuracy, most clients I've dealt with over the past three decades share the following common traits (in descending order of frequency):

- an attraction to the beauty of wood and other natural materials
- a strong appreciation for fine craftsmanship
- a good education, often at or beyond college level
- ample disposable income
- the ability to verbalize clearly, if not illustrate, the product they wish to have built
- a desire to interact with the craftsman behind the work

Where do you find these people?

Begin by looking in areas that have a strong tradition of woodworking, as these usually boast a large, appreciative group of potential consumers. The New England states; parts of New York, Pennsylvania and Kentucky; the upper Midwest; the northern coast of California and parts of Arizona and New Mexico readily come to mind. Regions with colleges and universities and regions with high-tech industries have proportionately large populations of people characterized by the traits listed above. Other areas of the country, because of outstanding beauty and attractions such as large ski or golf resorts, seem to attract that portion of the population having an enthusiastic desire to dispose of their disposable income.

For a region to be of interest to cabinetmakers, it must appeal to a promising clientele and offer prospects for future growth. You will not be employed for long if there is a dearth of homes into which to put your products. (As Neil Young so aptly put it, "You can't have a cupboard if there ain't no wall.") In general, the healthier the construction trade in a region, the larger the trade in custom cabinetwork.

The Marketplace

To develop a clear picture of construction activity in an area, look at the building permits issued over the past several years. These documents are public record; check the county's building or planning department. Search for a substantial number of large single-family homes with a high cost per square foot and for owners who are also listed as builders. These are good indicators of custom homes, which likely have custom cabinetry. Of course, a strong showing of kitchen remodels is also a promising sign. Talk with several realtors who list custom homes, and meet with a representative of the local builder's association; this should help complete the picture of a community's current vitality and give you some insight into the future.

If construction in a region is doing well, it's a good bet that there is considerable competition for the work (unless the growth is a recent phenomenon). While you should never give up because of an abundance of cabinetmakers in a region (I'll talk more about this in chapter seventeen), try to get a handle on the intensity of the competition. Divide the number of consumers by the number of suppliers. If the building permits reveal that 300 new homes were built last year and you assume they all procured their cabinets locally from the 25 cabinet shops listed in the local yellow pages, each cabinet shop had the potential for supplying 12 homes with cabinets. Unless these cabinet shops were all one-person operations, this is not good news. This kind of market analysis can be misleading, however, as not all custom work results from the construction of new homes and not all shops seek out custom homes. For shops geared to the high-volume production of modularized cabinetry, custom work is all too often a losing proposition. They make their money supplying tract homes and multiplexes.

To gain a more accurate feel for the competition, get out in the field and visit the cabinet shops oriented toward custom residential work. It won't take a Sherlock Holmes to detect how many are competing directly for your market, and how pressed they are to meet the demand.

To complete your understanding of a region's marketplace, research the types of products that are in vogue. Get a feeling for the area's prevalent trends in cabinet styling, configurations and finishes by visiting new homes for sale or viewing photographs of interiors on file at local real estate offices. Talk with local interior designers, residential architects and custom-home builders to broaden the scope of your inquiry. It is not necessary to be an absolute conformist to succeed in this business, but if the style of your work falls outside the current trends, you may need to rethink your product.

Product Definition

For the successful introduction of a product into a marketplace, it must have widespread recognition and appeal. If you were to insist on marketing traditional New England pine cabinetry in an area such as coastal California, the response would be innumerable blank stares. In that part of the country, a cabinetmaker is better off working in the style of traditional California craftsmen and designers such as Green and Green. In the far northwest of the United States, cabinetwork with a delicate, Japanese style finds widespread favor, as does the Taos style in the southwest. In my experience, it is far less frustrating (and more healthy economically) to either work within the parameters of a regional flavor or strike out and develop an entirely unique style. Don't waste your time trying to sell a traditional style that has as much local appeal as a fish stuck in a tree.

Once you develop a style that sells well and that you enjoy producing, stick with it. There are two good reasons to do so: product recognition and production efficiency. Before long, your shop and the work it produces will become synonymous in the collective mind of the marketplace. The continued production of an established product is necessary to avoid killing the goose that laid the golden egg. Production efficiency allows you to earn the butter for your bread. Efficiency cannot develop if you have to change setups and processes every time you get a job. Once you set up shop, your time should go primarily to the production of the product.

You have two more ways to define yourself and your product to the public. The first strategy is to specialize in one type of cabinetry, such as wall systems or kitchens. You can bill yourself as a specialist ("Mr. Kitchen" of the Hoboken Kitchen Design Center, for example) and focus production and marketing strategies to take full advantage of a narrow field of endeavor. The second strategy is to enter the market at the very top end. The competition is usually sparse for work at the leading edges of the market, but if your product doesn't truly belong there, you could end up running home with your tail between your legs. Since either of these strategies automatically reduces the pool of prospective customers, employ them only in a healthy marketplace with strong growth potential.

Price the Product

Having targeted the clientele and developed an appealing, well-built product, you must now price it fairly. Both overcharging the consumer and short-changing yourself are ultimately fatal errors. To price accurately, you must thoroughly understand the factors that determine a product's price. Then develop an estimating system that will quickly and accurately price the work in a way that maximizes its appeal to the client while minimizing compromise of your profit margin.

To determine the price of a product, first add the cost of the materials and shop supplies consumed to the expense of shop time and outside subcontracts. Next multiply this sum by a factor to produce a price equal to the profit margin plus cost. Sound simple? It actually can be quite complex. Let's take a close look at the components of this formula.

The materials cost is based on the

total amount of wood products consumed by the project. Add a 15 percent markup to account for production waste. Add to this the cost of fasteners, finishing materials and hardware. Shop supplies include materials consumed in portions (glue, filler putties, solvents and thinners) and disposable items (rags, sandpaper and throwaway brushes).

Determine your hourly shop rate by adding the shop overhead (computed per hour) to an hourly labor rate. To figure the shop overhead, refer to the expenditure ledger (see page 101), which accounts for most monthly expenses; if you are just starting up, use project expenses. Be sure to account for the following items: rent or mortgage; facility repair and maintenance; utilities, including telephone; business expenses such as insurance, office supplies and license renewal fees; vehicle expense (actual or based on mileage); bookkeeping and tax preparation fees; advertising and portfolio development; machinery maintenance; and such miscellaneous expenses as work clothing, laundry and hand-tool replacement. To be really accurate, go beyond the expenditure ledger and account for equipment depreciation and other losses, such as bad debts or projected inflation on basic shop expenses (including major tool replacement).

Determine the overhead rate by summing all the expenses incurred by the shop over a certain number of hours and then dividing by that number of hours. For example, if in one month of operation (160 hours) shop expenditures totaled $622 and the shop incurred $58 in depreciation and other losses, the shop overhead rate would be $680 divided by 160 hours or $4.25 per hour.

That was easy; the hard part is determining the amount of money you need to make an hour. If you are the head of a household and the shop is your family's sole source of income, you will need as high a labor rate as possible. If you are independently wealthy and think custom cabinetmaking is nothing but pure entertainment, you can reflect that in low prices or by sim-

ply working less for hire. For the sake of us householders, please refrain from the former and have fun with the latter — a woodworker's dream is to have time to build pieces on speculation.

The point is that the labor rate can range from zero to any number that will support you and your family. Of course, you must give to the business in relation to what you draw out of it. To earn a high labor rate without pricing your products out of the market, you must run an efficient shop and be one sparking spark plug in both the shop and the marketplace.

For example, assume you decide to draw $630 (before taxes) per week from the business; that is $15.75 per hour for a 40-hour week. Adding this $15.75 to the $4.25 overhead rate yields a shop rate of $20 per hour of operation. Knowing this figure makes pricing a particular product simple. If the materials for a hutch, including shop supplies cost $500, a subcontractor charged $150 for a set of doors and production of the hutch required 50 hours of shop time, the price formula would look like this: $500 + $150 + (50 × $20), resulting in a product cost of $1,650. Add profit if you want it; if you don't, your shop does. A profit margin provides capital for reinvestment, not necessarily for growth but for the upgrading of major stationary machinery. (Only the replacement of existing tooling is captured in the shop overhead rate, which includes loss due to depreciation.) In addition, the accumulation of profit cushions the shop through periods of production downtime caused by machinery glitches or your absence from the shop floor as you work on the books, talk on the phone and woo prospective clients.

The profit margin, like the labor rate, is rather arbitrary. Profit is not always linked solely to pricing, as profit can be generated by increased production efficiency and purchasing thrifty materials. I suggest, however, that you add a bare minimum profit margin equal to 15 percent of the product cost. Twice that amount is better if it keeps your pricing competitive. This extra

Determining Shop Rate Based on Monthly Expenses

Expenses Per Month

FIXED

Shop rent	$250.00
Waste collection and water	14.00
Equipment depreciation	58.00

AVERAGED

Shop maintenance	45.00
Telephone	30.00
Electricity	30.00
Business expenses	158.00
(insurance, licenses, office supplies, bookkeeping, advertising)	
Vehicle	95.00

Total overhead	680.00
per hour (÷160) =	4.25

Labor rate per hour	15.75
Total hourly shop rate	$20.00

JOB CARD	PROJECT NAME:

SPECIFICATIONS

Dimensions:	Wood type:	Special hardware:	Other:

MATERIALS					LABOR		
Date drawn	Qty.	Description	Price @	Cost	Date	Operation	Hours
		Waste factor on wood (15%)					
		MATERIALS TOTAL				TOTAL SHOP HOURS	

SUMMATION

SUBTOTAL MATERIALS			NET COST	
SUBCONTRACTS			PROFIT (margin _____)	
SHOP HOURS @ _____			PROJECT COST	

percentage will provide a cushion if you need to adjust your prices to meet market conditions. Going back to the hutch, adding 15 percent profit to $1,650 makes the price $1,897.50 (plus sales tax). To simplify the arithmetic, multiply the cost by 1.15 (price = cost + [cost × .15] = cost × 1.15).

Cost Estimating

While it is easy to figure out a product's cost after it has been completed, it's the rare customer indeed who will wait until the job is done to learn the bill amount. The custom cabinetmaker is doomed to give bids based on the basic specifications of a proposed project.

The key to making an accurate bid is a careful estimation of material and labor costs based on a structured assessment of previous work. This task is manageable if all the production data for every product built are carefully recorded on job cards designed for this purpose. I keep a copy of the job card shown on page 108 on the clipboard that hangs on my mobile tool caddy, Moe. Fill in the top of the card with the name of the project (usually the client's last name followed by a number if it's part of a larger project) and its specifications. (Include all external dimensions, the type of wood products used and any hardware other than the typical fastenings, hinges and drawer slides.) The balance of the job card is a ledger having two categories. The first describes the materials consumed in the project, including an estimate of shop supplies and their costs; the 15-percent waste factor appears at the bottom of that column. The second category lists the hours of shop time. The abbreviations shown on page 110 identify the production processes discussed in section two. The bottom area of the card gives the subtotals and gives the cost of the project.

For a tool to be effective, it must be used properly, and a job card is a tool. Use it habitually. Log all materials and the labor time of each process. Using a homemade timer (see page 111) is a great way to track elapsed time up to a total of 12 hours. Reset the clock to 12:00 at the beginning of each process and activate the timer with the switch. (The light indicates when the timer is counting.) When the process is completed, or anytime work is interrupted, switch off the timer. To prevent the desire to strangle wooden birds every 15 minutes, avoid cuckoo clocks.)

Pricing Formulas

Don't be surprised at how soon you appreciate the usefulness of job cards. Armed with a sheaf of cards, you can develop pricing formulas to accelerate the cost estimation process to nearly warp speed.

The formulas, derived directly from the information tabulated on the job cards, are based on the cost per square (or linear) foot of the products. In general, the standard lowers and uppers of kitchen cabinetry, as well as other varieties of cabinetry, can be accurately priced with a linear-footage formula. Larger cabinets (such as floor-to-ceiling oven units and pantries) and freestanding units (such as china hutches and entertainment centers) are more accurately priced using a square-footage formula based on the surface area of the cabinet face.

As an example, let's develop a formula for pricing out a $4\frac{1}{2}' \times 7\frac{1}{2}'$ kitchen hutch. Looking at a job card for a recently completed 4'-wide by 7'-tall china cabinet, we find that the total materials cost was $450 (including the 15 percent for waste) and total shop time was 100 hours (at a shop rate of $20 an hour). The cost of that project was thus $2,450 (= $450 + [$20×100]). Dividing this figure by the faces surface area (4' × 7' = 28 square feet) results in a per square foot cost of $87.50.

This figure, however, includes the china cabinet's doors and drawers: To arrive at a universal factor for pricing hutches, which will most likely be configured differently, doors and drawers must be treated separately. Referring to prior job cards reveals that a run of 20 drawers costs $200 in materials and $400 in shop time. Simply dividing $600 by 20 drawers yields a cost of $30 per drawer. A similar analysis of a door

Abbreviations of Production Process

Job preparation	C	Consultation
	D/C	Design and calculations
	M/H	Material handling
Sheet-stock sizing processes	Sht-C	Carcass panels (including backs)
	Sht-Dwr	Drawer components
	Sht-Dr	Door panels
	Sht-Shf	Shelves
Sheet-stock milling processes	Sht-Prep-C	Carcass components
	Sht-Prep-Dwr	Drawer components
	Sht-Prep-Misc	Miscellaneous sheet components
Solid-stock sizing processes	Sld-Face	Face-frame components
	Sld-Dwr	Drawer Faces
	Sld-Dr	Door rails and stiles
	Sld-Pan	Moldings
	Sld-Misc	Trim, edgings
Solid-stock milling processes	Sld-Prep-Face	Face-frame Ritter process
	Sld-Prep-Dwr	Drawer-face hardware preparation and edge treatment
	Sld-Prep-Dr	Edge treatment of rails and stiles
	Sld-Prep-Pan	Lamination of panels, final sizing, edge treatment, other milling processes
Component-assembly processes	Comp-Face	Face-frame assembly
	Comp-Dwr	Drawer assembly
	Comp-Dr	Door assembly
	Comp-Shf	Shelf edging
	Comp-C	Carcass panel edging
	Comp-Misc	Sub-unit assemblies (moldings, trim packs)
Final assemblies	Ambly-C	Case assembly
	Ambly-Face	Installation of face to case
	Ambly-Hwr	Hardware installation
	Ambly-Mld	Installation of molding and trim packs
Finishing	Fin-Prep	Sanding and scraping processes
	Fin	Application of finishes, including buffing out
Delivery	Del	Delivery
Installation	Inst	Installation of cabinet units
	Inst-Tm	Trimming out

run yields a cost of $24 per door. Since the china cabinet had two drawers ($60) and eight doors ($192), subtract $252 from the total cost of $2,450. Dividing this new figure ($2,198) by 28 square feet yields a cost of $78.50 per square foot of face; the universal factor for hutches. Thus the price of the $4\frac{1}{2}'$ $\times\ 7\frac{1}{2}'$ kitchen hutch under consideration can quickly be estimated as shown on page 112.

That's a handy system, but what do you do when the only job cards you own are the blank ones you just copied out of this book? When you are just starting out you have little or no data for calculating universal factors. You need to ascertain what the other boys on the block are doing. I'm not suggesting you get bids on a hypothetical project from your neighborhood custom cabinetmakers (you have to live with these guys). Instead, develop universal factors by analyzing the price sheets of a number of ready-made cabinets distributed in your area. To approximate custom work pricing, look at the models near the top of the line. Extrapolate figures for cabinets of various dimensions and configurations, with and without doors and drawers, to generate some pricing formulas. Use these until you collect enough job cards to produce your own formulas. Remember to update your factors continually as your production skills increase.

Write Bids

We've addressed presenting a quotation that specifies the contingencies under which the bid is written and how payments are to be made, but what about the bottom line — the one with the dollar figure on it? You must reveal your price sometime, but be sure you don't cut your throat when you do so. Few feelings are worse than when a prospective client takes one look at the bottom line and says, "Wow." You know at that instant that you have just either lost the job or your shirt.

Fortunately, you can write bids that won't cause such misery. Scrutinize the

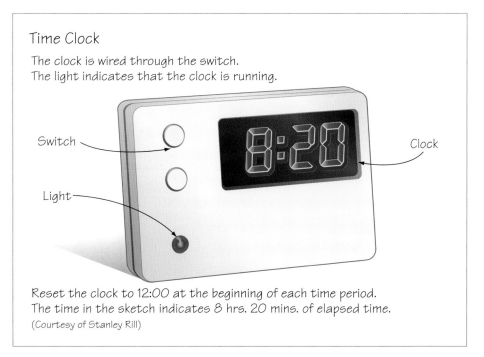

Time Clock

The clock is wired through the switch.
The light indicates that the clock is running.

Switch

Light

Clock

Reset the clock to 12:00 at the beginning of each time period.
The time in the sketch indicates 8 hrs. 20 mins. of elapsed time.
(Courtesy of Stanley Rill)

blueprints or drawings for every factor that could affect the final cost of the project. Account for all doors and drawers and any specialized hardware items, such as lazy Susans and slide-out baskets. Note cabinets with exposed end panels, because they cost more to build than those with unfinished ends. Record any unusual layouts that will affect construction methodologies and any dimensions that will produce a lot of waste in 4' × 8' sheet stock. While your nose is in the blueprints, make sure built-ins will fit through the site doors on installation day. (Second-floor bathroom vanities have been the Waterloo of many a custom cabinetmaker.) Also, since architects are not infallible, make sure the cabinetry will not cross windows or other wall openings. Once I caught this type of mistake too late. The client wasn't amused by the suggestion of installing a glass back on a cabinet that marched across an expansive picture window.

The worst job situation I ever encountered was the case of the house that was put on backwards. (Actually, it was the mirror image of the house intended for that foundation.) A mix-up of plans resulted in a "left-handed" home with a "right-handed" set of kitchen cabinets. Fortunately, we did find those cabinets a "right-handed" home eventually.

Consider some other factors before writing that final bid. If the project will demand an unusual amount of consultation or design, due to inherent complexity or an intransigent client, account for the extra time. Large projects require more time for the logistics of handling raw materials. If a project will include delivery, check the distance to and access to the site before bidding. As I mentioned earlier, never include installation of the cabinetry within the terms of a bid (unless you are forced to). If a project is done on a fixed price, installation is a certain way to nick your throat, if not worse. Finally, think about that profit margin. While a 30-percent markup is ideal, a lower margin might be in order if competition for the project is stiff or if acquisition of this job will lead to more profitable work. In the latter case, a lower initial margin will serve as the infamous "loss leader" that helps get your foot in the door. Going below a 15-percent margin, however, should be out of the question. You may win jobs, but they will not sustain your business. Remember, you work for yourself and for your shop as well.

ESTIMATION FORM	PROJECT: KITCHEN HUTCH

SPECIFICATIONS:
- 4'-6" x 7'-6" x 22" (lower)
  - 12" (upper)
- OAK THROUGHOUT

- 4 Flat recess-panel doors
- 2 Drawers
- Shelves open in upper

		FACTOR	
SQUARE FACE FOOTAGE or LINEAL FOOTAGE	33.75	18.50	624.38

ITEM	NUMBER OR FOOTAGE	FACTOR	
Doors	4	24.00	96.00
Drawers	2	30.00	60.00
Moldings	7 LFT. CROWN	2.50	17.50
	7 LFT. COVE	1.25	8.75

SUBCONTRACTORS		N/A
OTHER COSTS (freight, delivery, etc.)		30.00

HARDWARE

ITEM	QTY.	PRICE @	COST	
Drawer Slides	2	5.00	10.00	
Door Hinges	4pr.	6.00	24.00	
Shelf Clips	16	.15	2.40	
Levelers	4	1.95	7.80	
SUBTOTAL HARDWARE			44.20	44.20

SUMMATION		
	TOTAL NET	880.83
	PROJECT (margin 15%)	132.12
	TOTAL (plus tax)	1012.95

ESTIMATION FORM	PROJECT:

SPECIFICATIONS:

	FACTOR	
SQUARE FACE FOOTAGE _____		
or	_____	
LINEAL FOOTAGE _____		

ITEM	NUMBER OR FOOTAGE	FACTOR	
Doors			
Drawers			
Moldings			

SUBCONTRACTORS		
OTHER COSTS (freight, delivery, etc.)		

HARDWARE

ITEM	QTY.	PRICE @	COST	
	SUBTOTAL HARDWARE			

	TOTAL NET	
SUMMATION	PROJECT (margin)	
	TOTAL (plus tax)	

17 | market and sustain the business

When marketing a line of high-quality custom cabinets, you must understand that you are selling yourself as well as your work. As mentioned, the consumers of these products are not motivated just by the beauty of wood and the quality of the construction. They are drawn to the opportunity to interact personally with you, the craftsman. People expect a true craftsman to reflect the qualities inherent in his or her work. You are expected to be as creative and exacting and honest and durable as the cabinets you build. Your task is to meet those expectations in how you present yourself to your clients both in your business media and displays and in your personal etiquette.

Business Media and Displays

Business cards and stationery are your emissaries to the marketplace; they should reflect your dedication to quality and hint at your creative talents. Use eye-catching graphics but avoid cartoonish, timeworn depictions of hand tools or furniture. In design, simplest is often best, and no harm can come from simply stating your name and occupation and the location and phone number of the shop.

At right is a collection of effective business cards. Although Dale West's card is simple, its all-text design is tasteful while his mission statement of "uncompromising craftsmanship" gives potential customers an ample heads up about what to expect from his work. The Huey's card is also simple but striking because of its dramatic color contrast. Michael Morrow's card uses bold colors and artwork to stand out and a statement that succinctly sums up his business. Bruce Kieffer's card offers a more general statement, though the photo of the unique vanity dresser leaves no mistake about his products. Claude Boland's card similarly uses a portfolio photo (though more as a watermark) and makes its mission statement by implication: a photo of a cabinetmaking ancestor. Finally, Ernie Baird uses a line drawing of a traditional boat from a widely seen photo that has graced boating event posters and CD covers around the Puget sound area for years to inform the type of boat work his shop specializes in. The well-known boat was built by Ernie.

Use the same logo and typeface for your business card and your letterhead. Although not essential, personalized business stationery used to communicate with clients and trade professionals helps foster the impression of a meticulous, committed craftsman who means business.

Do not use or distribute your business media indiscriminately: Placing business cards at local restaurants and bowling alleys is a complete waste of time, and using company stationery for personal communication is a waste of a rather expensive material (and it smacks of showmanship). Your business media should be used primarily to identify you to present and potential clients, and to lend credibility to your communication within the trade.

The rest of this chapter deals with ways of getting the market to open its doors to you. Once it does, you must have something besides your good looks and a business card to show off. I recommend preparing a portfolio of photographs and a sample case, which represents your work in three dimensions.

My present portfolio is composed of about twenty 8" × 10" color photographs that present an overall view of installations and about twenty 5" × 7" photos highlight the details. (Although projected slides are more impressive than

An Overcrowded Business Card

HANDCRAFTED WOODEN CABINETRY
European Master Craftsman
15 Years Experience

* Cabinet Design and Construction, All Styles
* Built-Ins and Freestanding Units
* Kitchens and Bathrooms
* Installations
* Antique and Furniture Repair

FREE ESTIMATES
Excellent References
914-525-0822

John Doe
222 Fog Road
Littleville, NY 00000

prints, the hassle and time involved in presenting them are real obstacles.) In the early days of my career, when the pickings were slim, the criteria I used to select portfolio candidates were somewhat less exclusionary than they are now: As long as I wasn't embarrassed by it, any piece could be included. Although the portfolio was rather small, the pictures were very good. Prospective clients will judge the quality of your work by the quality of your pictures, so consider investing in professional photography for your portfolio. Freestanding pieces are especially responsive to professional studio treatment.

Even the best photography won't survive shoddy presentation, so forget about stuffing the photos in your kid's Marvel comics folder. Buy a high-quality portfolio case from the local office supply store. Ideally the case should hold each photo in a glare-free sleeve. Each sleeve should be loosely attached to the binding for easy adding and reshuffling of photos. I like to caption each photograph with a title such as: "East Wall, Hargrave-Garrison Kitchen." Going to these lengths reinforces your image as a creative, meticulous and detail-oriented craftsman.

A nicely constructed sample case, which is just a miniature cabinet on a swiveling base (see at right), will accent the "highly skilled" facet of your public image. This cabinet can feature a number of different door and drawer styles; provide examples of face-frame and European-style cabinets; and demonstrate drawer slides, door hardware, adjustable shelf clips and adjustable legs (with clip-on kickboards). The sample case stores wood samples and a selection of miniature doors that represent other available styles. Do your best work in the creation of this case, but use standard materials and procedures in its execution. It is, after all, a representation of the product you offer to the marketplace. Don't include hand-cut dovetails in rosewood drawer sides unless you intend to offer such features in your production units.

This sample case is actually a miniature standard cabinet module. The sides display different styles of doors and drawer faces and pull hardware. One face is operational, opening to reveal a miniature drawer, an adjustable shelf and a slide-out. Don't get carried away with extraordinary details on your sample case; it must honestly represent your production cabinetry.

Build Relationships Within the Trade

A custom cabinetmaker's work often comes through referrals from architects, interior designers and custom builders. For this reason, you should cultivate relationships with as many of these professionals as possible. When developing a list of potential contacts, begin with architects as they can offer referrals to other members of the trade. Since the work of many architects carries them far from the world of custom woodworking, you needn't call on every one of them. Eliminate any listed under "industrial designers" and "project management" in the yellow pages. Screen the remaining architects with a simple telephone introduction: "Hello, I own Woodchuck Woodworking. We specialize in high-quality custom cabinetry and wonder if you have anything on the boards that might require this kind of product." Most architects will respond with a straightforward yes or no. The ones who respond immediately with a firm yes are usually involved in a residential or commercial design where they have some control over the selection of subcontractors. These are your hottest prospects; respond with a brief rehearsed soliloquy about yourself, then request an opportunity to show your portfolio and sample case. A reserved yes usually means the architect is designing for builders who handle their own woodworking or subcontract it. All is not lost, however, as architects are usually willing to name local general contractors who specialize in custom-home construction or who use custom woodworking elsewhere in their businesses. Architects have nothing to lose by offering the names of their clients, and you have everything to gain by growing your network of contacts.

Begin screening this select group of contractors by telephone. Mention the name of the referring architect, then ask whether any of the projects currently under construction or in proposal will have bids let out for custom cabinetry. If the answer is positive, recite your introductory soliloquy and request an opportunity to show your sample case and obtain a copy of the blueprints for the project. Many contractors will say that they already have shops they feel comfortable dealing with, but they will be open to meeting a new guy. Take advantage of this; you can be pretty comfortable to work with, too.

Some architects may offer names of interior designers. Introduce your products to them as well. You'll find, however, that most interior designers have little to do with interior woodworking and custom cabinetry. They are primarily contracted to choose and coordinate wall and floor coverings, fabrics, furniture styles and other decorative aspects of interiors. You may just find a designer who's involved in built-in furniture designs and kitchen layouts and is happy to learn of craftsmen who can provide well-built products.

Contact Cards

Before long, you'll be inundated with the names, addresses and phone numbers of contacts and contact referrals. Follow up on all of these, and develop a system for organizing the information and keeping it up-to-date. On a card like the one below, contacts are put into four categories: architects, interior designers, general contractors and owner-builders. There is also space to write in the source of the referral. (You can always get a toe in the door if you mention the name of a contact's colleague when introducing yourself.) Use a series of columns to record the sequence of any transactions; be sure to date each transaction and indicate its

A Contact Card

CONTACT:

REFERRED BY:
Architect   Interior Designer   Contractor   Owner
(Circle one)

ADDRESS

TRANSACTION ABBREVIATIONS

PHONE (home) _____
       (office) _____
       (site) _____

NA - No Answer   MA - Made Appointment
LM - Left Message   MR - Made Referral
CB - Instructed to call back   UD - Update

TRANSACTIONS

	1	2	3	4	5	6	7	8	9	10	11	12	13	14	15
DATE															

REFERRALS:

nature using the abbreviations provided. Never leave a dated transaction column blank. If an appointment is made, write it into a separate appointment calendar immediately. If referrals are offered, note them on the card and fill out a new contact card for each name.

Appointment Etiquette and a Pep Talk

When scheduling a business meeting outside the shop, avoid Mondays. Everybody is recovering from the weekend and wondering why they are at work; don't make them wonder why you are there, too. Fridays are also bad. Everyone is anxious to go home; don't be one more reason why they can't yet.

Having arranged a potentially lucrative meeting, make the most of it. Be punctual. If you must cancel the appointment, or if you run late call as soon as possible and reschedule. Such courtesy is noted and appreciated, and it makes a good impression before you even show up. Dress in clean clothes you keep for these occasions, but don't overdo it. You are a woodworker first and a businessperson second. Avoid suits; a casual sport coat is fine.

With an impressive portfolio in one hand and a sample masterpiece in the other, you have some heavy artillery for any business meeting. Avoid two thoughts that could damage that valuable first impression. The first: "My work stinks compared to the work of a lot of other people around here." A good way to respond to this thought is to acknowledge its truth. Nearly every woodworker at some time meets somebody whose work is better; those who feel they are the best may have ceased to appreciate and learn from the work of others and it shows. The other damaging thought: "With so many other woodworkers out there, how can there possibly be room for me?" Of course you won't know unless you try, but chances are there's plenty of room at the inn. Remember you are the woodworker currently meeting with this particular client. The opportunity for you to be in the right place at the right time puts you light-years ahead of those craftsmen who are hiding in their shops (even the ones whose work is somehow always better than yours).

Once in the meeting, be polite. Introduce yourself via an orchestrated journey through your portfolio. The photographs will provide a stimulating visual backdrop as you intone your resume. Make your sojourn as entertaining as possible, offering quips and interesting (but brief) sidelights to the material being presented. At the end of your portfolio, turn the spotlight on your sample case. Let your host open and close the doors and drawers of the case; he or she will discover the door and wood samples stored within. Questions and comments will invariably result, and the prospective client will take over the show. Very likely the subject of his or her own work will come up, and you should encourage this. When the time looks right, steer the conversation toward current projects on the boards and under proposal. This gives you a chance to evaluate the job potential of this particular contact.

Conclude the meeting by affirming whatever follow-up seems appropriate. If the potential for work is imminent, suggest another meeting, perhaps with your host's clients present. Even if the potential rewards of this meeting seem far off, say you will stay in touch, then keep that promise. Do not join the crowds of shop-bound woodworkers, forever lost to the contacts that you have just begun to nurture. Before exiting, hand over several of your business cards and extend thanks for the meeting. If you have a Web site that features sample photos and testimonials on your work, be sure to mention it and to point the address out on your card.

Don't dawdle; sweep yourself out the door before the secretary tries to sweep you under the rug. As soon as possible, write down everything pertinent to the meeting. Log on the contact card the follow-up, note if other forms of follow-up are necessary (such as sending copies of photos in your portfolio), fill out new contact cards for any referrals and enter subsequent appointments onto your calendar.

Direct Marketing to Consumers

A large portion of your work probably will come through direct contact with consumers. Through relationships with trade professionals, you may receive direct referrals to their clients. These are always good prospects, as their names would not have been released unless they had reserved the right to contract for their own cabinetry.

Another way to find these owner-builders is to comb through recently issued building permits at the county's planning department. If a project is to be built by the owner, the permit will say so. A more convenient strategy may be to join the local builders association; up-to-date listings of building permits often appear in their newsletters. There are, of course, other benefits to joining these organizations, not the least of which is the dissemination of your name among a receptive group of tradespeople.

About once a month, peruse the permit data and send a business card and standard letter of introduction (see the sample next page) to promising prospects. The postcard mailer shown on page 120 is another excellent option. Select the lucky recipients of your communication based on the category of the permit, the value of the project per square foot and the location. In my own estimation, if the category is residential, the value of the project reflects an above-average investment and the location is in an area of high land values or other custom homes, then I've found a hot prospect. After sending the letter or postcard, wait about a week and follow up with a phone call. Politely ask if the prospect received your mailing and whether he or she wants to meet with you to discuss the project further. He or she will probably say no. Don't be surprised; the rate of positive return on any kind of marketing strategy is, almost without exception, far less than 10 percent. Prospects will tell you they have already hired a cabinetmaker or they are doing the cabinets themselves with the jigsaw they got for Christmas (don't laugh) or they are planning to order cabinets from Home

A Direct-Marketing Letter

Dear

I recently learned through the local builders' grapevine that you are contemplating, or have already begun, the construction of a new home or remodel. If you are interested in obtaining competitively priced, well-built cabinets for your project, you might wish to consider the services of a local custom cabinetmaker.

Employing the skills of a local craftsman allows you to obtain products that will be carefully designed and constructed to meet the specific, demanding requirements of your unique project. Nearly any configuration of cabinet can be constructed, and any of the wide variety of cabinet woods and specialty hardware items can be incorporated into the design. The choice is up to you.

I would be pleased to show you a portfolio of my work, which encompasses twenty years of supplying fine homes with fine cabinetwork in styles ranging from the strictly period reproduction to the uniquely contemporary. Please feel free to call and arrange for an appointment. I look forward to meeting you, and I wish you well on your project. Thank you for taking the time to read this letter.

Sincerely,

Depot. For the one in twenty who says, "Yes, I'm glad you called," pull out a fresh contact card; fill in the name, phone number and address (and the site address, if different); and indicate in the transaction column what the next move is to be. If a meeting is planned, note it on the contact card and on your appointment calendar.

Whether to meet prospective clients at their home (or the site) or in your shop is generally left up to you. Most people, however, will express a desire to see where you work. As we discussed earlier, the public seems to carry a universal image of the venerable woodworking craftsman, and they are curious to see one in action. Don't disappoint them; invite them to your shop.

Schedule the meeting to take place during a logical break in your workday, such as at lunchtime or immediately after quitting time. Try to have the shop somewhat neat so your prospects won't trip over wood scraps, but leave some hand tools out to satisfy their expectations of Geppetto's workshop. Once they arrive, give them the shop tour and briefly mention your work in progress. As in your meetings with the trade professionals, your big guns are your portfolio and sample case. Steer the clients to the office (if you have one) and make them comfortable. Offer a beverage, and then jump right into the show.

You can determine quite a bit about your prospects by the questions they ask. If they all relate to money, heed the caution light in your head; these people are less interested in your product than in what you charge for it. This doesn't necessarily mean all bets are off. It can simply indicate they are pricing out the various components of their new home. In this case, spend less time on product information and get right down to the bottom line.

It doesn't hurt to bring up the subject of money. In fact, I usually tell people the approximate prices of the projects shown in the portfolio. I can then judge from their reactions how serious they are about investing money in their dream cabinetry. Don't try to shatter these dreams, but don't get yourself into a nightmare, either.

I am usually wary of the prospective client who concentrates solely on the work and shows absolutely no interest in the price. While it might appear that the ideal money-is-no-object consumer has come to your door, this person is probably just there to pick your brain and get some free ideas. Never write off a prospective client with whom you meet; simply arrange to develop a bid for the project. If the client cannot leave a set of plans, arrange for copies to be made at a print shop where you have an account. The copies can be left for you to pick up at your convenience. (Clients usually pay for the copies, but if they're charged to your account, you will likely pay less than you would to mail the original prints back to the client.)

Be prompt with any quotation, and send it with a note on another business card thanking the prospective clients for coming to your shop. Don't hold your breath awaiting their response; it may take months, or it may not come at all. Following up the quotation with a phone call is not necessary. If the job is yours, which is all you really want to know, they will tell you in due time.

A Postcard Mailer

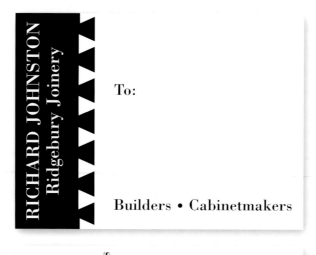

Advertising Avenues

Many people in the trades say that trying to find work through advertising is a dead end. In my experience, they are mostly right, especially about paid advertising. However, nearly everyone puts things inside cabinets. If you are just getting started or have moved your shop, it is worth trying to reach people through advertising.

The least expensive (but not free) advertising is a classified ad in the local newspaper. You can spend a little more money for a display ad, but I don't believe these are more effective. Newspapers usually offer a price break to long-standing advertisers (which is the only effective way to use this kind of advertising) and often provide a separate column for service listings, including cabinetmaking. See if you can get them to add custom to the title. For a while, you may be the only one listed under this heading.

The ad I usually run is shown on the next page. It contains only 16 words plus a phone number, yet it conveys enough information to introduce the products I make. Placing my name and occupation in bold print at the beginning of the ad leaves nothing to chance. Over an extended period of time, the classified readership subconsciously links that name to cabinetmaking. This will occasionally produce an inquiry; but don't pin your hopes on it.

Another way to buy advertising at a reasonable rate is to list your business in various regional yellow pages. For people who are new to an area or who have no source of referrals, the yellow pages serve as a credible introduction to the service community. If your name is there, you may get a call. Always ask callers where they got your name; learn which of your advertising dollars have some effect.

Probably the most effective advertising is the kind you don't have to pay for. I call it indirect advertising, anything that ties your name to your work. Most communities offer a host of opportunities for this type of advertising. You can participate officially in community events that enjoy high public visibility, such as parades and fairs. You can donate shop time to local nonprofit endeavors. If you have the inclination, you can teach woodworking on a volunteer basis to kids, or for pay to adults at night school. For a number of years, I opened my shop several evenings a week to six amateur woodworkers. I charged by the hour for the use of the shop, throwing in advice and occasional instruction at no extra charge. Numerous referrals and subsequent jobs resulted from these contacts. I've also helped build playground equipment, parade floats and small boats (for raffles). Any of these activities can help make your name synonymous with your work and can set you up for a feature story in the weekend edition of the local newspaper.

Also consider joining the local chamber of commerce and other business organizations that promote local industry. This will enhance your credibility as a business entity within the community, and participation in these officially sanctioned groups will also spread word of who you are and what you do to a large number of professionally and socially active people.

A Good Reputation

The most important asset that a person can acquire in this business, other than a mastery of vocational skills, is a good reputation. When you are perceived by the community as having this near-mystical quality, your security as a self-employed craftsman is greatly enhanced. This esteemed stature becomes the only form of advertising necessary to attract a steady flow of business to your shop. You can groom a perception within your community that you do, indeed, have a good reputation. The secret lies in learning how to conduct yourself around the people you work for and those you work with.

I must admit that I have at times paid dearly to keep the "good" in my good reputation. Indeed, I have found a great deal of truth in that old maxim that proclaims, "The customer is always right," even on the occasions when I knew I wasn't wrong.

With almost every client discrepancies somehow slip between the cracks of mutual understanding: times when a drawer will not be where it's supposed to be or when proportions of full-scale moldings do not match the client's expectations. I find that the best way to handle these situations is simply to correct the "error" if it can be done without a major expenditure of additional labor. This allows the clients to feel that you are truly concerned with their happiness.

On any job, one of your goals should be to leave the clients feeling good about you and your work. Remember that you are pleasing not just this client but all those clients in your future. In the end, it is great to have former clients speak highly of you to their peers, beneficial if they speak of you at all and absolutely deadly if they speak ill of you. The effects of ill will at the end of a job last long and reach far, and are far more detrimental than swallowing a little ego and eating some humble pie. If you are careful with the written agreements, you should never have to eat too heartily.

You'll likely be relieved to hear that there are less-stressful ways to help make a client feel good. Be courteous when customers walk into your shop but also be attentive to why they are there. While there is a limit to the amount of time you can take away from production without charging for it, your clients need to feel at ease talking with you. My own rule is that when the visit moves beyond 15 minutes, it's time to blow the whistle and schedule a paid consultation. If an unannounced, unknown visitor comes to your shop, graciously suggest scheduling a meeting at a mutually convenient time. If the inquiry begins to resemble a consultation, mention your consultation fees — that should separate the wheat from

A Classified Ad

the chaff.

As subsequent client meetings take place, always show interest and respect for their ideas on design, layout and, heaven forbid, construction techniques. You may be surprised to find that some of their ideas are even workable. In any case, your clients should feel that you share their enthusiasm and excitement about their kitchen, breakfront, etc., and that you are proud to be a party to its creation. Remind yourself that no matter how many kitchens or other projects you have done, this particular one will be unique and dear to the people who have entrusted you to build it. After all, if they didn't feel so strongly about their furnishings, they wouldn't have come to you, the master custom cabinetmaker, in the first place.

Having received a deposit and begun working on a project, stay in close touch with the anxious owners-to-be. At appropriate stages, invite them to the shop to view progress. Allow them to share the excitement of creation; this will also help them to remember to pay the installments without prompting.

When the project is finally complete and awaiting delivery, call your clients in for a viewing. Before they arrive, cover the work with a clean white sheet. This conveys to them that you are protecting the piece from the perils of the workplace, and it adds to the drama of the unveiling. This viewing allows everybody to discuss and enjoy the completion of the project free of the usual hustle and tension of installation. Again, do what you can to promote good feelings.

When installation time arrives, observe the basic rules of etiquette. Avoid damaging your clients' doors, floors, carpets or poodle(s). (I have done in one of each over the past 30 years.) Protect vulnerable areas with drop cloths or moving blankets (the latter can be rented, and often purchased, at local U-Haul outlets). Give the poodle a bone and lock the dog in the bathroom. Before leaving, vacuum and wipe clean everything you touched and put everything you disturbed back in its place. The only evidence of your presence should be the professionally installed project. If the project is a kitchen, try leaving a fresh bouquet of flowers on the sparkling new countertop. Remember to leave several business cards tucked in the flatware drawer — and to let the mutt out of the bathroom.

Follow Up

Summoning the energy to follow up on a completed job can be hard to do, but it's definitely worthwhile. A month or so after the project has been completed, when your clients have had time to live with the work, call them and ask how everything is going. Chances are excellent that everything will be just fine. (If they aren't, you will hear about it in less than a month.) This follow-up phone call will be appreciated and will reinforce your clients' perception that you care about the quality of your work and their satisfaction with it. What a superb way to turn a former client into a future client.

Working for the Generals

In new homes and large remodels, you may find yourself working for a general contractor. Maintaining a good reputation with this breed of client requires a different form of etiquette. Leaving flowers for the general will not work.

Establishing a relationship with a contractor is less a matter of achieving personal rapport then it is of striving to be a useful cog in the machine that built Jack's house. That machine is a merry-go-round. On it you will find plumbers, electricians, painters, wallpaper hangers, stairmakers, tile setters, Sheetrockers, carpet layers, carpenters, architects, owners and six different radios set to six different stations. Your job here is to become a good carousel horse, running like mad in one place and never getting in anyone's way. To this end, it helps to enlist the golden rule of subcontracting: Take your orders from the general, but do nothing until you've talked to the other subs first. These are the people who you will actually have to work around (and over, under and beside). Be assured that if you work well with the other subcontractors on the project, you'll look just fine to the top gun. His or her primary concern is that the job as a whole progresses smoothly, so don't stop the music (in fact, bring your own radio).

It pays to keep the army of subs happy with you as well, since you will probably find yourself working around them again. Remember that all subcontractors are essentially in the same business and that work for one tends to lead to work for everyone else. I always look forward to installation time and the sharing of bad coffee and even worse humor with other tradesmen whose respect I have earned.

Working With the Team

It may be clear on your contract who is paying you, but this is not necessarily the person who will be making critical decisions about the job. On larger projects, the decisions concerning your piece of the pie might be made by any number of people, including the general contractor, the architect, the interior designer, the finish subcontractor and the owners. At any given time, who should make a decision largely depends upon the aspect of the project under question. The owner (if there is more than one, make sure they speak with one voice), in conjunction with the project's designer, should have the final say on matters concerning layout, design details and options called for in the final approved drawings for the project. If you were not the designer, be sure you are clear who was. If a correction affects another subcontractor, inform the general contractor immediately.

In reality, almost any change that occurs after the final drawings are approved is likely to affect everyone. It's imperative that those involved in the direction of a large project meet on a regular basis to keep the work on course. This is the only way you can be assured that any change orders you receive (you already know they have to be in writing) are understood and approved by the people who are affected by them. If you suspect that the orders haven't been seen by everybody (I've been on a number of jobs that were undermined by interpersonal hostilities), go up the chain of command and ask. Questioning orders properly will do your reputation no harm, but getting caught in the middle and blamed for a change that should not have been made can do you a world of harm.

epilogue

Our work as independent custom cabinetmakers is a relatively rare phenomenon in the 21st-century world. As we are apparently becoming a nation of consumers for the rest of the planet, the number of people who derive a livelihood from the creative use of their minds and hands will likely continue to diminish. Custom cabinetmakers will not likely ever be included on charts that list growth industries.

Yet the humane value of participating in an occupation that walks tenuously between the handicrafts of the last century and the electronic revolution of this one can hardly be judged by its impact on the gross national product. The work that we do is truly important. The lifestyle that comes to us through the nature of this work nurtures and enriches us, and I trust that the products that we build and sell to our neighbors will enrich their lives as well.

appendix 1
tools and supplies

Here's where you can find the specialized items mentioned in this book:

*Cabinet jacks and wax kit
(for plugging nail holes):*

FASTCAP
888-443-3748
www.fastcap.com

*Hole guide for router; edge
trimmer guide for router:*

MEG PRODUCTS
609-587-7187
www.megproducts.com

*Pocket screw tools
and fasteners:*

KREG TOOL COMPANY
800-447-8638
www.kregtool.com

High-quality hand tools:

LEE VALLEY TOOLS
P.O. Box 6295, Station J
Ottawa, Ontario
Canada K2A 1T4
US: 800-871-8158
Canada: 800-267-8767
www.leevalley.com

BRIDGE CITY TOOL WORKS
920 NE 58th Ave., Ste.100
Portland, OR 97213-3786
800-253-3332
www.bridgecitytools.com

*Tormek water sharpening
system, sliding table for table
saw, splitter for table saw insert, miniature power feeder,
edge-banding machine, ceiling-
mounted air filter, drill press
table and clamp system, back-
to-back clamps:*

HIGHLAND HARDWARE
800-241-6748
www.tools-for-woodworking.com

**ROCKLER WOODWORKING AND
HARDWARE**
800-279-4441
www.rockler.com

WOODCRAFT
800-225-1153
www.woodcraft.com

Wood sample box:

EDENSAW WOODS, LTD.
360-385-7878; 800-745-3336
www.edensaw.com

Kitchen design software:

KITCHENDRAW
613-692-0193
www.kitchendraw.com

KCDW SOFTWARE
508-760-1140
www.kcdw.com.

*Cup hinge installation tools
and hardware:*

BLUM
800-857-8721
www.blum.com

Kitchen accessories:

BLUM
800-857-8721
www.blum.com

**CABINET ACCESSORIES
UNLIMITED**
800-667-8721
www.kitchensource.com

HAFELE NORTH AMERICA, CO.
800-423-3531
www.hafeleonline.com/usa

FEENY MANUFACTURING CO.
P.O. Box 191
Muncie, IN 47308
765-288-8730

REV-A-SHELF
P.O. Box 99585
Jeffersontown, KY 40269
800-626-1126

appendix 2
further reading

Books and Information on Starting and Operating a Small Business

Small Business Start-up Kit by Peri Pakroo. Nolo Press 2004.

The Partnership Book by Denis Clifford and Ralph Warner. Nolo Press, 2001.

Marketing Without Advertising by Michael Philips and Salli Rasberry. Nolo Press, 2003.

Publications of the Small Business Administration

Websites: www.irs.gov/businesses/small or www.sba.gov

National Association for the Self-Employed: www.nase.org

Books on Shops and Tools

Setting Up Shop by Sandor Nagyszalanczy. Taunton Press, 2000.

How to Design and Build Your Ideal Woodshop by Bill Stankus. Popular Woodworking Books, 2001.

Mastering Woodworking Machines by Mark Duginske. Taunton Press, 1992.

Books on Casework Design and Processes

Making Kitchen Cabinets by Paul Levine. Taunton Press, 1988.

Designing Furniture from Concept to Shop Drawing by Seth Stem. Taunton Press, 1989.

Building Cabinet Doors & Drawers by Danny Proulx. Linden, 2000.

Other Books by Jim Tolpin

Building Traditional Kitchen Cabinets. Taunton Press, 1994.

Built-In Furniture. Taunton Press, 2001.

Jim Tolpin's Table Saw Magic. Popular Woodworking Books, 2003.

appendix 3
production flowchart

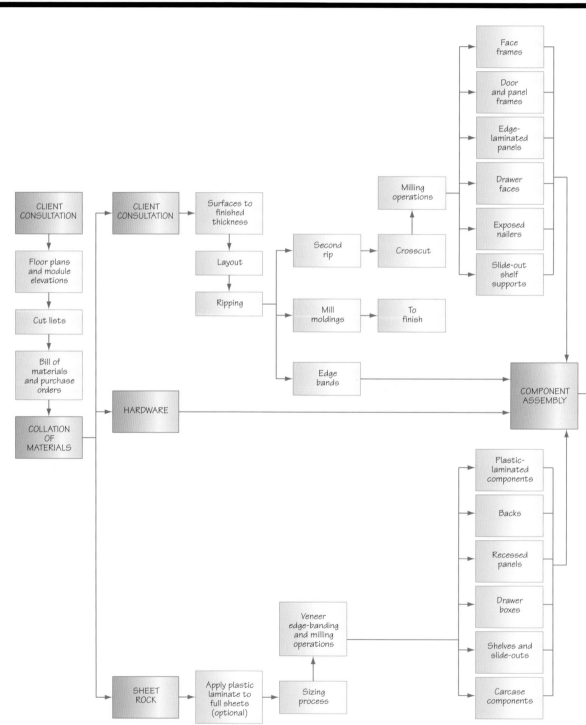

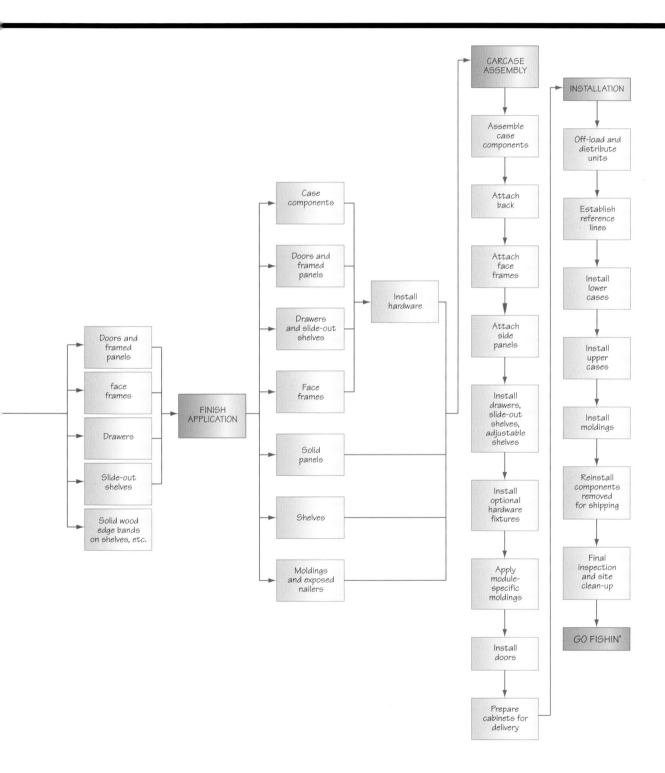

index